WHAT REALLY MATTERS

Harmensz van Rijn Rembrandt, The Return of the Prodigal Son, 1668–1669. Hermitage, St. Petersburg, Russia. *Scala/Art Resource, NY*

Also by Arthur Kleinman

Writing at the Margin:
Discourse Between Anthropology and Medicine

Rethinking Psychiatry:
From Cultural Category to Personal Experience

The Illness Narratives:
Suffering, Healing and the Human Condition

Social Origins of Distress and Disease:
Depression, Neurasthenia and Pain in Modern China

Patients and Healers in the Context of Culture:
An Exploration of the Borderland Between Anthropology,
Medicine, and Psychiatry

What Really Matters

Living a Moral Life
Amidst Uncertainty and Danger

Arthur Kleinman

OXFORD
UNIVERSITY PRESS
2006

OXFORD
UNIVERSITY PRESS

Oxford University Press, Inc., publishes works that
further Oxford University's objective of excellence
in research, scholarship, and education.

Oxford   New York
Auckland   Cape Town   Dar es Salaam   Hong Kong   Karachi
Kuala Lumpur   Madrid   Melbourne   Mexico City   Nairobi
New Delhi   Shanghai   Taipei   Toronto

With offices in
Argentina   Austria   Brazil   Chile   Czech Republic   France   Greece
Guatemala   Hungary   Italy   Japan   Poland   Portugal   Singapore
South Korea   Switzerland   Thailand   Turkey   Ukraine   Vietnam

Copyright © 2006 by Arthur Kleinman

Published by Oxford University Press, Inc.
198 Madison Avenue, New York, NY 10016
www.oup.com

Oxford is a registered trademark of Oxford University Press

Library of Congress Cataloging-in-Publication Data
Kleinman, Arthur.
What really matters : living a moral life amidst
uncertainty and danger / Arthur Kleinman.
p. cm.
Includes bibliographical references and index.
ISBN-13: 978-0-19-518098-5   ISBN-10: 0-19-518098-4
1. Conduct of life—Case studies. I. Title.
BJ1547.4.K54 2006
158—dc22
2005031823

1 3 5 7 9 8 6 4 2

Printed in the United States of America
on acid-free paper

Contents

Note to the Reader

nformation contained in this book accurately conveys the spirit of my work as a physician and researcher, but, with the exception of the historical chapter on W. H. R. Rivers and my own autobiographical details, all names, characteristics, and identifying details in the case histories have been changed. This is meant to ensure confidentiality and protect the anonymity of the individuals, families, and institutions involved. When I have made such changes, I have drawn on information from other patients and research subjects facing similar problems to make the alteration valid in the light of the moral experiences of people I have treated and studied and lived among as a whole.

For Gabriel, Kendall, Allegra, and Clayton Arthur.

For Anne, Thomas, Peter, and Kelly.

For Joan.

For Marcia.

For Steven, Lee, Julie, and David.

For Laura.

For this family moving through ages and worlds . . .

WHAT REALLY MATTERS

1

Introduction

What Really Matters chronicles stories of ordinary people and what matters most to them, in normal and extraordinary times. It is a book about moral experience and how individuals and groups come to grips with danger and uncertainty. We tend to think of dangers and uncertainties as anomalies in the continuum of life, or irruptions of unpredictable forces into a largely predictable world. I suggest the contrary: that dangers and uncertainties are an inescapable dimension of life. In fact, as we shall come to understand, they make life matter. They define what it means to be human. This is a book about people who, in the midst of such challenges, are trying to live a moral life.

The phrase "moral life" can be ambiguous because *moral* can be used in two different senses. In its broader meaning, the word *moral* refers to values. Life, in this sense, is inevitably moral, because for each and every one of us, life is about

the things that matter most to us. Just carrying on our existence, negotiating important relations with others, doing work
that means something to us, and living in some particular
local place where others are also passionately engaged in these
same existential activities—all this is, by definition, moral
experience.

But this meaning of *moral* is not synonymous with *good* in
an ethical sense. The moral experience that people share could
be far from good, even malign. The values that we express and
enact can be inhuman. Think of a local community that scape-
goats or oppresses a minority, or one that supports slavery, child
prostitution, violence toward women, or other abuses. Here
one's moral experience could include complicity in terrible acts,
just as ordinary men and women were caught up in perpetrat-
ing the Shoah or racial slavery. Normal and shared moral experience of this sort is so troubling precisely because what looks
so wrong from the outside (or from the victim's perspective)
may not look that way from the inside, from the perspective of
collaborators and perpetrators. That is why, in this first sense,
what is moral needs to be understood as what is local, and the
local needs to be understood to require ethical review (scru-
tiny from the outside and from those on the inside who challenge accepted local values).

In its more focused meaning, *moral* refers to our sense of
right and wrong. When we say we want to live a moral life,
we mean one that embodies our own moral commitments.
We can imagine a certain way of conducting our lives that
seems right: we can feel responsibility for others, and act on
those feelings; and we can respond to trouble and those in
trouble in a way that makes us feel we are doing good in the

world. We expect that other people in very different locales would agree that these acts are moral in this second sense, and even if we do not receive approbation from others, we feel ashamed if we act in a way that goes against this core impulse to do the right thing.

Those who seek to live a moral life may develop an awareness that their moral environment, in the first sense, is wrong. They may respond with criticism, protest, and personal efforts to do the right thing, no matter how great the odds against them being effective and how likely it is that their choices will have negative consequences for them. Many will not rock the boat, and their interior, moral life will reflect the problems with moral experience surrounding them. This is how people come to collaborate publicly with unethical policies, in spite of their private reservations, and later on develop feelings of guilt and misplaced loyalty, while others stay in denial for a lifetime. Of course, there are other people who seem tone deaf to moral sensibility, who appear to be unmoved by feelings for other human beings. We shall see that moral life is closely connected to the idea of ethics, by which we mean we aspire to values that transcend the local and that can guide us in living a life.

Can we learn anything from the stories of people who have tried to live moral lives in very different settings, amidst particular kinds of dangers and uncertainties, that can help us do the same? Is it really feasible to try to live in a way that runs against the grain of the moral environment that surrounds us? When there is real uncertainty about what to do and when the level of danger is high enough to threaten what really matters to us, what kinds of decisions do we make?

Ordinary experience frequently thrusts people into troubling circumstances and confounding conditions that threaten to undo our thin mastery over those deeper things that matter most, such as our self-esteem, intimate relations, or religious values. Divorce, the death of a loved one, injustice and discrimination, dead-end jobs, unemployment, accidents, chronic illness, artistic failure, alienation from faith community: any of these common calamities can break our grip on what we hold dear, and destroy our sense that we are in control of our fate.

A surprising number of American families go into bankruptcy, about one in every seventy-five households this year, and a very large number just barely avoid it, constantly living on the edge of financial insecurity. A middle-aged executive in New York has a heart attack and is unable to continue working. His disability creates a new and dangerous financial reality for his wife and young children and causes him to question the meaning of the life he has built. A young Bostonian loses her job as a software developer and cannot find a new one; her sense of self plummets, and she becomes depressed and suicidal. A struggling working-class African American family in New Orleans loses its beloved only son in Iraq, and months later their third-generation family home is destroyed by Hurricane Katrina. The boy's father, a recovered alcoholic, refuses to seek a substitute for the rehabilitation program he has participated in for several years and goes on a binge of drinking. A liberal, professional Palestinian husband and wife, both educated in Paris, are shocked by the horror of a brilliant daughter, a high school honor student, killing herself and others as a suicide bomber at an Israeli bus stop and leaving behind a video in which she rejects secular values and commits herself to the fundamentalist religious ideal of jihad. These are but a few illustrations of the danger and uncertainty that surround us and could strike us at any time. Readers will doubtless be aware of others close to their own lives. On an even larger scale, the evening news reminds us regularly of natural and man-made disasters that can overturn life at a moment's notice. Tsunamis, earthquakes, and hurricanes can destroy whole cities and kill or uproot hundreds of thousands of people. Failed or corrupt states in Africa or Asia, famine, or civil war visit misery on countless others. Terrorist attacks in New York, Madrid, London, or Jerusalem unleash horror in the midst of the most prosperous cities. A rash of deaths from avian influenza raises the specter of pandemic disease that could touch anywhere on the globe.

But immediate threats to a comfortable existence come at a much more intimate level: within our own bodies. For all of the medical breakthroughs of the last fifty years, for example, most people are aware that many health problems are incurable and that most of us will face the pain and limitations of chronic conditions. Even a short list feels too threatening to think about: diabetes, heart disease, ulcers, multiple varieties of cancer, asthma, lupus, hepatitis, kidney failure, osteoporosis, Alzheimer's. Not to mention that time itself saps our energies, disfigures our bodies, and increasingly slows and muddles our thought processes. And death, a silent haunting of our days, waits for each of us.

Even in the absence of tragic events or disabling illness, people struggle steadily throughout their lives to hold on to those things that matter most to them, things such as status, jobs, money, family ties, sexual intimacy, sense of order and self-control, health, life itself, and also religious commitments, political arrangements, and all sorts of culturally and personally specific agendas. This daily struggle can be fierce and desperate because it is inevitably unequal. There is a powerful, enervating anxiety created by the limits of our control over our small worlds and even over our inner selves. This is the existential fear that wakes us at 3 a.m. with night sweats and a dreaded inner voice, that has us gnawing our lip, because of the threats to what matters most to us.

WE EMPLOY A VARIETY of strategies to deal with the profound sense of inadequacy and existential fear bred by the limits of our control. There is outright denial with feigned nonchalance. There is, for those who can afford it, a comfortable boredom laced with escapism: "Forget about life for a while." There is, for a happy few, an irrepressible good humor. There is fatalism, as voiced by Harvey Deaton, a survivor of the terrorist bombings in London on July 7, 2005, to the *New York Times:* "If your number's up, your number's up." And there is the hormonal surge of youth, searching for physical challenges from bungee jumping to other extreme sports—substituting the frisson of immediate but containable risk for the far grimmer reality of distant but uncontrollable perils.

Magical belief in technological supremacy over life itself is yet another classic American cultural coping response, as is facing only problems that reach the crisis level one at a time. And financial advisors, insurance salespeople, surgeons, psychological counselors, security experts, and many other professionals have a vested interest in selling the comforting but fundamentally misleading notion of certainty about control over human affairs. "Risk management" is yet another society-wide myth that is punctured every time catastrophe—from hurricanes to epidemics—strikes us unprepared. These cultural responses work by deluding us as to the nature of the human condition.

Given the manifest shakiness of our lives, what is surprising is that we act, think, and write as if we were in control of ourselves and our world. It is our assiduous denial of existential vulnerability and limits that is extraordinary in American culture. Much of our society, of course, is founded on a myth of self-control (Jefferson's perfectibility of man), mastery of the environment (taming the frontier), beneficence of our social order (the city on the hill), and denial of human limits, including the ultimate one, death itself. Our pervasive consumer culture is founded on another myth of control— the belief that we can solve our problems through the products that we purchase. Politics and the entertainment industry likewise hold out the promise of easy solutions that minimize the reality of danger and uncertainty. But although such cultural myopia may reach its extreme here, it is not just American capitalism that underwrites denial. Socialist societies find it equally unacceptable to take too dismal a view of the human condition and its possibilities. Even most mainstream religious traditions today have moved away from earlier visions of the precariousness of the human condition to embrace at least some aspect of the big lie. It is as if modernity itself were predicated on fostering this fiction, a falsehood at the center of global culture.

YET IN TIME most of us are forced by the sheer recalcitrance of the world and the appreciating fragility of the body to face up to the size of the odds against us. We often camouflage it by humor and irony, which seek to keep the dark reality of it at a distance, and we muddle through clinging to the basic common sense that on any given day we are likely to make it home safely. Of course, we need to do some amount of self-blinding just to function. If one had to review each day the "thousand natural shocks that flesh is heir to," in Shakespeare's words, one might never get out of bed. In that sense, denial of how chaotic and unstable life really is would seem necessary and healthy. Yet when the denial becomes so complete that we live under what amounts to a tyranny of not seeing and not speaking the existential truth, it becomes dangerous itself. This is what makes the closest and deepest experiences of catastrophe, loss, and failure so terrifyingly unsettling. We puncture the bubble of illusion and cannot find our footing. We become disoriented because we see the world in so new and fierce a way.

This is not to say that our lives are nothing but a sequence of defeats and miseries. Each of us knows triumphs from time to time. Especially among those whose resources (financial, educational, and social capital, as well as health and emotional well-being) offer greater protection against the exigency of threatening life events and the wearying pressures of existence, aspiration and successes are realities. And especially when we are young, life offers many joys and delights. Deep investment in family, work, friendships, creative opportunities, and the building of futures makes it easy to forget the grim burden of threat and loss. When we are young, we also simply don't have enough of those crucial experiences of bereavement, anxiety, and failure to teach us the bleaker side of existence. Neither heroes nor monsters appear in most lives. But over time most of us come to know at first hand the trials that make living such a serious business. Most victories such as job promotion, financial success, and seeing a creative project realized are transient and limited in extent. Lives can be rich with beauty and happiness—and in well-off countries or neighborhoods many people enjoy both—yet as one ages ostensible good fortune is often tempered, if not overbalanced, by disappointments, unfulfilled hopes, and the indignities of aging. Beyond the immediacy of a joyous occasion, the periodic yet magical feeling of ebullience, and even long-term happiness and the sheer distracting routine of one darn thing after another lies what the great American psychologist and philosopher William James called "genuine reality." And it is life's trials—bad luck, suffering, and even calamity—that teach us endurance and acceptance of genuine reality.

Today, our view of genuine reality is increasingly clouded by professionals whose technical expertise often introduces a superficial and soulless model of the person that denies moral significance. Perhaps the most devastating example for human values is the process of medicalization through which ordinary unhappiness and normal bereavement have been transformed into clinical depression, existential angst turned into anxiety disorders, and the moral consequences of political violence recast as post-traumatic stress disorder. That is, suffering is redefined as mental illness and treated by professional experts, typically with medication. I believe that this diminishes the person, thins out and homogenizes the deeply rich diversity of human experience, and puts us in danger of being made over into something new and frightening: individuals who can channel all our desires into products available for our consumption, such as pharmaceuticals, but who no longer live with a soul: a deep mixture of often contradictory emotions and values whose untidy uniqueness defines the existential core of the individual as a human being. When this happens, the furnishings of our interior are no longer the same; we are not the same people our grandparents were, and our children will not be the kind of people we are. Several of the cases in this book reveal this disturbing trend. The fear seems to be pervasive that if we admit what our condition is really like, we will fall apart, both as individuals and as a society.

But after three decades of doing psychiatry and anthropology, I don't see any convincing evidence that facing up to our human condition leads to paralysis and pathology. Quite the opposite, as the stories in this book illustrate: seeing the world as dangerous and uncertain may lead to a kind of quiet liberation, preparing us for new ways of being ourselves, living in the world, and making a difference in the lives of others. Surprisingly, confronting the deepest fears can mean giving them up and asking critically why we ever allowed ourselves to be so morally and emotionally shackled.

Many of the highest attainments of civilization have come from those who have had the courage to peer unflinchingly into the darkness of reality. Since the time of the ancient Greeks, the Western literary genre of tragedy has wrested remarkable wisdom from the encounter of human beings with the fierce and unyielding way things are behind the façade of convention. Just to think of Antigone or Lear is to understand how we have been enriched by this countervailing force. Rembrandt's *Prodigal Son*, which appears on the cover of this book, is a beautiful painting, yet its beauty is saturated with a sense of suffering and loss at the heart of life. Rembrandt's work links the aesthetic tradition with religion as perhaps the most powerful means by which we build ethical meaning out of adversity and failure. This is also much of the substance of the Book of Job and the Gospels, as well as the texts and rituals of Buddhism, Hinduism, Confucianism, Taoism, Islam, and many of the world's folk religious traditions. They reveal the truth about how easily our sense of comfort and order is shaken and how hard we have to struggle to maintain our identity and cultural worlds in the face of profound suffering. Yet it is in that struggle—as Antigone, Lear, and Rembrandt's figures so poignantly illustrate—that we find the meaning of our humanity.

THIS UNBLINDED PERSPECTIVE on life is voiced by many people I have met in research and clinical settings over the years. Thus, one informant, who at the time was a fifty-two-year-old unemployed executive in New York City with serious coronary artery disease, put it this way: "You grow up in [American] society and you kind of get lulled into the view that you are protected, things are easy. You can take life easy. Then something happens, and . . . you come to see just how dangerous things are. I've had it happen several times in my life, so I should be prepared. But the only preparation is to be wary . . . all the time. That's why over time you stay very attentive to things at work, in the neighborhood, even in the family. Even in your body. I've been laid off after twenty years with one firm. I've been in a bad, bad car accident. I've experienced the death of a daughter to suicide related to drugs. And now my heart problems. The world is a dangerous place. Maybe even more dangerous than I'm willing to admit."

Another research interviewee, this time a sixty-eight-year-old Chinese intellectual in Beijing in the 1990s, reflecting on his life experience in a very different cultural environment, told me: "My grandfather told it to my father during the warlord period. My father told it to me during the war with the Japanese. And I told it to my son and daughter during the Cultural Revolution. He understood it, but what could he do? He was murdered. Even in these prosperous times I'm sure my daughter tells my granddaughter: Be careful! Be very careful! Times change. History changes. The world is not the same. But social life is always very dangerous."

Those who have lived through the sort of experience these men speak of have felt life transmute into something new and different, something not altogether understandable or desirable; they have felt danger and uncertainty in their bones. A seventy-five-year-old French academic, responding to a question about what he had learned by living through the German occupation of France, through the immediate postwar period with its cultural movements of existentialism and abstract expressionism, through the student protests and extreme political polarization of the late 1960s, then through the era of unbridled commercialism and centrist political and cultural blowback of the 1980s and 1990s, with its anti-immigrant and antiglobalization populist movement, and finally through the new time of Islamist terrorism, ruefully observed: "This is a strange world, Arthur! You cannot predict what is ahead. I feel, like many of my circle, more and more estranged by what is happening. It is like I am watching one disaster after another unfold. This world of ours is a very dangerous place. If you can lift your ideas beyond the ordinary and see the way the world is and what we are and who we are becoming, you cannot honestly say to yourself . . . you understand what is happening. It is . . . you feel alien, or rather the world feels that way. That way and frightening."

"Oh, come now, it's always been bad . . . if you look deep into it," interjected his wife of forty years, a painter and daughter of Holocaust survivors. "Isn't that so? So we just look away like the plowman in Auden's *Museé des Beaux Arts*. If you look under the rug of civilization, where it's dark and wicked, we are fierce and terrifying. You need to face that to discover the possibility for creating something better," she whispered.

These very different individuals from quite different societies insist that modern culture contains a big lie. By failing to acknowledge the omnipresence of hazards, we maintain a false image of who we are. And if we are misinformed about who we are, then how can we prepare for where we are headed and what lies ahead? I hold, as do the protagonists of these three vignettes, that if we can learn to face genuine reality, we can live better. That is the purpose of this book.

I do not mean to suggest that confronting genuine reality means seeing only the worst of experience. Joy, exuberance, and fulfillment are just as real as the darker and more perilous moments upon which I am focusing our concern. Love and hope are not negated by loss and threat; if anything, they become better understood and more deeply cherished. It is the sentimentality of Hollywood (and Bollywood) films with their happy endings that look truly misleading when placed against the truth of experience. The artists I spoke of earlier, who explore the depth of tragedy, show us just how precious and hard-won are our real victories. Look again at Rembrandt's *Prodigal Son:* the reunion of the father and son is suffused by a glow of true joy, which is all the more radiant because of the years of pain plainly etched on the old man's face. Living a life embraces positive and negative conditions, and indeed is a story of how they come together. Enlightenment about genuine reality should not demoralize us; it gives meaning to our small triumphs and daily pleasures.

The fact that selves and world can be reworked in response to hazard and insecurity, and that they are worth remaking, in spite of their limits, is what makes aspiration so important. To experience the limits of living and the inevitability of being checked in everyday practice is not to be defeated or to despair in ethical, religious, or aesthetic ways. Ethical, religious, and aesthetic work remakes the actual practices of ordinary life, forging new synergies between values and emotions, so that individual and collective significance, transcendence, and the sense of ultimate order and control come to animate who we are. It is precisely when an individual, a family, or a community is threatened by catastrophe that people turn to religion for explanation. They seek support for their deepest values, succor for the existential feelings of loss and dread, and revival of hope. Religious rituals, and relationships with coreligionists and religious leaders, do just this. They revivify what really matters. Failure and catastrophe empower religion; religion, in turn, empowers people faced with adversity to overcome self-doubt and fear of failing, and to act in the world. Is it surprising that the current period of Christian reawakening and evangelical fervor intensified in the wake of September 11 and America's global war on terrorism? There is also a downside to religious responses to existential threats of catastrophe. We know that suicide bombers include many whose religious zeal in the face of what they perceive to be a threat to Islamic values calls them to their destructive acts, and dangerous religious passions also motivate hatred and killing amongst Hindus, Buddhists, Christians, and Jews who mix fundamentalism with nationalism.

Culture expresses our sense that there is a special essence to all that is human, and therefore that each of us is individually exceptional. Consider the large-scale cultural processes in Europe and America that followed the devastation of the world wars and the Shoah. Creative movements that united aesthetics and ethics went on to reframe human meanings through modernism, existentialism, abstract expressionism, Holocaust literature, and other literary and artistic movements. These created new ways of making sense of our chaotic and destructive world. They found value in people's individual lives at a time when a huge question mark hung over established cultural forms, calling into doubt their legitimacy and relevance. Even if the tone of the works was bitter, the mode ironic, and the ethical stance one of an isolated person facing a dehumanized void, the very process of creating beauty and order out of pain and suffering reinvested the world with human meanings. In this sense, these artistic and ethical creations rebuilt the world. Even in our complex era, when cultural energies in secular society have come to emphasize salvation through the body and its desires, there is a reimagining of who we are and where we are headed that revitalizes, once again, core existential values. You may find your way in being reborn to another world under the evangelist's tent; I may find mine in this world, planing the sea in my powerboat; we both may appreciate abstract paintings that resonate with our sensibility of what worlds are possible. Yet in existential terms these are simply different ways of aspiring to and actually creating order out of disorder and beauty out of jeopardy, new realities of meaning to sustain and recharge our hope in life.

For many, the most unsettling awareness of our times is the threat of anonymity. When we consider the small and forgettable quality of our private lives, we fear for the significance of our individual selves, our close connections, and our local communities. Does it really matter that we were here at this time? Will anyone remember us after we go? We fear an absence of our presence. Once again, our sense of being special is expressed and affirmed by religious, ethical, and aesthetic activities, which connect our private world to the larger one. That interior world is where we feel vitally alive and our lives convincingly carry unique significance for loved ones, shared communities of faith or artistry, and, not least of all, ourselves. And that is how we prevent cynicism and nihilism that would otherwise paralyze social commitments and individual initiative; that is how we nurture humor, optimism, and the common sense that we will somehow muddle through; that is how we preserve an enduring taste for life. Whether this cultural response is profound or shallow is less important than that it renews our sensibility to life itself. It allows us to savor our mundane existence. Instead of a gray grimness that arises when we coldly contemplate disenchanted human ends and discover just how much we can endure, we can revel in the thrill of color and sound, the charm of taste, the exhilarating lightness of touch, the rightly acclaimed mystery of love.

My point is that acknowledging the always unequal struggle between where the world is taking us and where we aspire to go does not at all mean accepting a glum perspective; rather, it involves developing a deeper and more fine-grained appreciation of what the moral experience of communities and the moral life of the individual are about, and why both are so important. Within this broader moral context, we want to know what we can learn to help us live a life. For this reason, it is especially instructive to examine the gray zones where the separation between acts that sustain a moral life and inhuman ones that destroy it is thin, because these zones of the most troubling moral experience show just how difficult it is to live.

In the course of our individual lives, moral and emotional experiences can change us so greatly that we are not the same people we were earlier: life, with all its transformations, has restyled us at the core. So, what is the core? Who are we? We need to get away from the idea of an unchanging human nature that resists all the myriad changes around us, like steel piers holding up a bridge in deep, rough water. That image holds for bridges but not for people. The countervailing image that arises in the mind is from the New England coast, where my family and I spend summers on the Gulf of Maine, above a large tidal river about two miles from the Atlantic Ocean. It is sometimes placid, sometimes very rough in these waters. Here the shoreline has a prima facie consistency, rocky ledges and rock-strewn beaches; if you are a serious boater, you have to be cautious, no matter your knowledge of hazards well marked on charts and your GPS. Owing to the tidal conditions and occasional great storms, things that have a seeming permanency—rocks, underwater obstacles, channel-marking buoys—can shift, sometimes substantially enough for a local lobsterman with two decades' experience of the water to run a thirty-two-foot lobster boat aground. If you regularly watch the shore, you see that it is under almost constant change, albeit within limits set by the local geology and hydrology. So with the self, the soul. The limits are set by the principles and empirical reality of biology and psychology. The self is moored by the neurobiological hardwiring of rude sentiment and the rough genetic scaffolding of personality. But there also are moral and affective currents constantly at work changing the self's topography. Neurotransmitters create rough sensations of pain and anger. Remorse, regret, and other complexes of emotions and values are strongly influenced by interpersonal relations and meanings that contribute to the building of the subtle and elaborated sensibilities that constitute who we are. And culture, politics, and economics transform each of us—if not from day to day, then from year to year as jobs change, careers transmute, families undergo growth and collapse, marriages rise or fall, and the large historical forces that shape the destiny of nations and influence entire populations roll over our lives, grinding, wearing away, shifting, breaking, making us let go and move on.

Danger arises when our most deeply held values and emotions are threatened or lost. And people themselves become even more dangerous when they feel that these things are at serious risk. Then they are frequently prepared to do anything and everything to protect and defend what really matters. In these moments of intense pressure, the self can be reshaped: the most placid and pacific person can become violent, can participate in oppression or crimes against humanity. Pogroms against Jews, from the Middle Ages up until the great Russian pogroms of the 1880s that drove hundreds of thousands of Jews to emigrate to America, not infrequently took this character. Fear of social disorder and major political change, laced with rumor, targeted a stigmatized "other" for destruction. A deadly epidemic, some other public catastrophe, and political dissension so threatened the local population and the central authorities that the Jews became a handy scapegoat. The Shoah—the genocide of European Jewry—can also be seen in these terms: ordinary Germans accepted the Nazis in order to stave off the Soviet menace and as part of the devil's bargain tolerated the Nazis' war against the Jews.

The willingness of ordinary Serbs and Croats to participate in the mass killings of Bosnian Muslims also can be traced back to the same social dynamic: a real danger threatening the moral order—in this instance, the breakup of the nation-state into warring ethnoreligious groups—is associated directly with the other group or indirectly blamed on them. This leads to the second-order, and often more deadly, danger of the threatened group either actively carrying out or passively acquiescing to the destruction of the people perceived as the source of that threat. The existential message is chillingly clear: we will do all that needs to be done to protect our way of life and ourselves, and if we perceive a serious threat, we will engage in violence as a preemptive strategy or even a kind of anticipatory revenge.

We can glimpse this social logic in the ways we Americans have responded to the September 11 attacks on America with the follow-on war on terrorism and the Iraq war. The toppling of the Taliban and the destruction of al-Qaeda training camps in Afghanistan made sense to many Americans, as did the international hunt for terrorists and their sources of funding. But the invasion of Iraq, its occupation, and the subsequent deadly mix of insurgency and civil war there suggest that we have gone too far and created just the kind of violent overresponse that I have pointed to as a second-order and greater danger. We seem to have a newfound certainty that vengeance is right, no matter how many thousands must die to avenge our national tragedy and affirm our national myth that we are making the world safer. We also have become so preoccupied by our fears of internal insecurity and hidden enemies that we have been willing to limit or actually abrogate constitutional safeguards of the very rights we preach as most sacred. Seen from this perspective, our quest for homeland security, our desire to mete out justice through vengeance, and our concern for global social control seem to matter more to us than our commitments to rights, legal procedure, and even the global democratization we proselytize so robustly. The last looks more and more like a fig leaf camouflaging those fiercer commitments.

As we continue to pursue these policies, which many Americans view as morally justified, we are accused by millions of Muslims of conducting a war on Islam, and by millions of Europeans and Asians of making the world more dangerous. Islamic communities provide moral support to young Muslim men and women whom we call terrorists and they call holy warriors and martyrs. Suicide bombers view their own horrific actions as morally just, and so do members of their networks and communities. So here we have a contest between radically different moral justifications.

If we step beyond our own taken-for-granted commitments and those of our adversaries, it is clear that the moral vision and commitments of terrorists, including suicide bombers, are utterly unethical and antihuman. But it should be equally apparent that our own lived values as outlined above, and as represented in how we behave in the world, are problematic as well. Neither moral position is acceptable. Both are perilous. To move beyond them we must advance an ethical approach that seeks to transcend local commitments and yet at the same time is locally applicable. To be effective at the collective level, such an ethical approach, I argue, must also work for the individual who is seeking to build a life. That is one of the things I seek to explore in this book.

The chapters that follow set out stories of the struggles to live a moral life of men and women I have encountered in my professional career as an anthropologist, psychiatrist, and China scholar as well as through personal friendships. Like the rest of us, these individuals have found themselves caught in particular circumstances and in cultural conditions where the things that matter most to them have been challenged by what is at stake for others or for society. For example, a former decorated soldier, now decades into a successful legal career, looks back on the atrocities he committed in the Pacific war and sees indelible evidence not only of his own moral failings but of society's hypocrisy in being unwilling to recognize that war is about turning ordinary men into killers. Once the transformation has occurred and violence is unleashed, society turns its back on the moral life of the perpetrator. The central tension between one person's ethical aspirations and society's moral reality extends for this angry middle-aged man into a conflict with his psychiatrist about what depression and its treatment are about. Is tragedy a disease requiring an antidepressant medication? Is a lifetime secret of having committed a terrible abuse a medical problem or a moral one? Are there moral disorders and moral therapies? Are remorse, regret, and repentance, not just symptom relief, the appropriate healing outcome for facing up to moral failure?

A liberal Protestant minister who is barely able to control his own sexual impulses experiences the selling of sex in the media and on the streets as an existential threat to moral responsibility, his own and his adolescent parishioners'. The fundamental conflict between religious aspiration and sexual reality (society's and his own) is experienced first as the conversion of guilt into excruciating bodily pain and afterward as the transfiguration of pain into the holy. His story will lead us through an exploration of living a life in the uncharted territory between religion and medicine. And a Chinese physician and intellectual confronts the political perils of the Cultural Revolution as a direct threat to his ideals, his family, his career, and his own life. He comes to understand, in the radically different era of economic reform, that an ethos of compromise, acquiescence, and readiness to deceive and exploit create a world in which living a moral life is intensely difficult as well as risky.

While the circumstances and conditions and outcomes diverge, all of the protagonists in the chapters that follow are caught up in moral experiences that define what it means to be human, forcing them to confront who they are but also provoking them to come to terms with who we all are, what our shared humanity is all about—albeit with an intensity that makes their life narratives arresting. I write these cases to illustrate how malleable moral life is, for individuals and groups—and to show just how central jeopardy is to our worlds and ourselves.

Can studying the experiences of a few individuals shape our responses to the challenges we will have to face? Because many of the challenges I review seem unmasterable, what is the implication for how we face them?

The answer is just that: we need to begin by surmounting our own denial and affirming our existential condition. Such crises and limits cannot be mastered, in the sense of conquered. They are to be understood and responded to as ethical, religious, and aesthetic challenges. Getting a handle on what really matters for us requires a self-critical stance toward our emotions and values in which we try to step aside from (or, really, outside) our taken-for-granted world and sense of self. No easy thing, but it can be done. Seeing ourselves in this way, we can ask the hard question: does what really matters for us contribute to an adequate or good life? If the answer is no, we obviously are in for a tough time of trying to remake our commitments and realign them to those surrounding us in our local world. If the answer is yes, then we still need to discover what the obstacles are to achieving an adequate life, and which (if any) of them can be surmounted. Even when the answer is that these barriers are the existential limits we face, the possibility is there to live creatively and morally. Even under threat to our core meanings, we can, for instance, first do no harm to ourselves and others. We have seen how first-order dangers, those forces outside ourselves that threaten what matters most to us, create second-order dangers, the threat within ourselves that in defending what we value we violate our humanity. Breaking this cascade can be a powerful way to transform ourselves and even our worlds—for example, by ending cycles of revenge, or by controlling anger turned inward into self-injury. By opening up a space of critical self-reflection on our world and ourselves, we can prevent ourselves and others from becoming worse people under the pressure of changing conditions. We can protest and resist a dangerous moral ethos in our families, workplaces, and communities, and even if we are unsuccessful at changing our local worlds, which is not unlikely, we can keep our moral practices in line with our sense of what is right. And that is indeed something worth struggling for, something that can transform others as well.

In several of this book's stories, the lesson is that squarely facing failures in life is as important for our worlds and the others in them as it is for our own self-esteem. We are morally responsible for ensuring that others understand the social injustice our worlds routinely create, including what we have brought about through our own actions. And we are also responsible for doing something about injustice.

In one story, we learn how AIDS transforms a mother and artist from a "taker" into a "giver," and we thereby see how existential crises caused by a health catastrophe can create a new moral life. In another of the book's cases, we learn how a formerly quiet intellectual moves out of the library into the public world of others' pain and suffering, so as to undo the very moral conditions that made him famous, but which he has come to understand are the cultural basis for political and medical disaster. The lesson is not one of standard heroism—there is no victory—but a kind of negative heroism or anti-heroism that may not change the world but helps make clear to others what needs to change if the world is to be a less unjust and desperate place. That antiheroism legitimates, at the same time, alternative ways of living in the world that offer new and different personal answers to the question of what an adequate life is. Heroic acts that change society are rare and more often than not meretricious fictions, whereas protest and resistance as well as perturbing and disturbing the status quo are, at best, the most ordinary people like us can achieve.

THESE CHAPTERS point to a new way of conceiving of ethics. *Ethics,* a set of moral principles that aspire to universal application, must be seen in a context of *moral experience,* which is always changing and usually uncertain, in order to provide a more adequate vision of values in society and how to respond to their clash and change. Taken alone, ethics, such as principles of virtue and justice, can be irrelevant to our local worlds, just as local moral experience, such as discrimination and oppression carried out in the interests of the dominant group, as in the American South in the era of segregation, can be unethical, even downright evil—and can render people unable to criticize their own conditions. I examine efforts to unite the two, moral experience and ethics, in the stories of actual individuals' lives. Individuals' efforts to live a moral life in the particular circumstances of moral experience can lead them to formulate ethical criticism of those circumstances as well as to aspire ethically to values that go beyond the local reality and seek universal support. This new framework for examining actual lives shows us who we are and who we can be in response to some of the more disturbing value questions of our era.

I include in these accounts an autobiographical chapter about times in my life when I too faced the issues of moral imagination and responsibility highlighted in the other chapters. This effort at self-knowledge signifies that the author cannot claim a position that is outside the local context of societal changes and moral struggles. I too have my own story to tell about moral experience and trying to live a life, as does each of you.

What we see in these stories, I believe, is not nearly so much the moments of intensive moral reflection that philosophers emphasize but rather what anthropologists and social historians, biographers and psychotherapists so often describe: the insecurity of moral life and the terrible inadequacy of our usual fumbling efforts to change or fully comprehend who we are and where our world is taking us. Yet, in the midst of it all, we make a life. So how does that happen? How do we deal with the world and build ourselves as moral agents? This is the existential core of each chapter that, I suggest, lies beneath cultural difference, social diversity, and personal uniqueness. This is what matters most to me. This is the book's claim to truth.

2

Winthrop Cohen

W inthrop Cohen represents for me the despairing idea
that society can impose on us a way of living that un-
leashes our anger and aggression in a thoroughly inhuman
way. He also represents for me the inspiring idea that the ordinary person over the course of his or her life can protest
that unethical imposition and can even insist on devoting a
life to remorse, regret, and repentance. Winthrop Cohen holds
another crucial significance for me. His case pointedly asks how
ordinary unhappiness and clinical depression differ. What does
it mean for us and our world when the soul's tragedy is diagnosed as a mental illness and treated medically?

I met him in a clinical consultation more than twenty-five
years ago. More accurately, I first met Mrs. Julia Richardson
Cohen and her married daughter, Alexandra Frost—both tall,
attractive, conservatively dressed, and worried. Winthrop had,
at the last minute, backed out of accompanying them.

"So what's the problem?" I asked mother and daughter.

"He won't talk about it," Mrs. Cohen told me. "Says he can't. But it is eating him up inside. I married a vibrant, wonderful man. Now he seems so sad, so hurt. It's not right. He's been so successful. We have everything anyone would want. So why does he seem so unhappy, so terribly unhappy?"

Mrs. Cohen's daughter added, "He's all closed up. We love him. He loves us. But we don't talk. Because he can't tell us what hurts so very much. But we're afraid, afraid for him." Then they both broke into sobs.

When they composed themselves, they told me they were quite sure Winthrop would come to see me, because he loved them and knew they were desperate for him to receive professional care. And indeed he did keep the next appointment several days later.

A short, stocky, immaculately attired, sixtyish man with a military bearing—straight back, shoulders squared, sitting bolt upright at edge of his chair, hair in a brush cut, speech clipped, but otherwise expressionless—Winthrop Cohen made no effort to contradict his wife and daughter.

"They're probably right. I accept all the responsibility. It's my fault."

"What's your fault?"

"The way I am, I guess."

"What way is that?"

"Ah, what to say, huh? Where to start?"

He sighed—long, slow, and very deep. He looked down at the floor. His face fell into a desperate sadness that made him look greatly vulnerable. It was now clear why his wife and daughter were so worried. He seemed on the verge of collapsing. I waited. After what seemed like a two- or three-minute pause, he cleared his throat, bit his lip, and began.

"The war. It's what happened to me in the war. I could never get over it. But I learned to live with it. Then all of a sudden on my sixtieth birthday it became a terrible weight. I couldn't put it out of mind. I feel so very depressed about it. Sometimes I sit for hours, brooding over the past. What I saw, what I did. My daughter calls it depression. I don't know what it is. But whatever it is, it is bad."

Winthrop Cohen had run away from home in a working-class section of lower Manhattan to join the Marines. The year was 1942. He was eighteen but looked older. After several months in training camp, he was shipped out to the Pacific theater. By the time the war ended, he had participated in the invasion of four islands including Okinawa, been twice decorated for bravery, and sustained two wounds, both visually impressive. One, a thin burn on the left side of his face, high across the cheekbone, extended from under his eye almost to his ear. It had turned lighter than the rest of his facial skin, which had a ruddy complexion, and had the effect of making him seem fierce and piratical, yet also aristocratic. The other, a long, deep, dark, dense scar on the outer surface of his right arm from wrist to elbow, a shrapnel wound, made me think of the kind of work injury a construction worker might fall prey to. Those two contrasting images—elite and blue-collar—created my sense of what Winthrop was about.

He was demobilized in 1945, after which he returned to New York, attended college on the GI Bill, received a scholarship to law school, and moved to the West Coast, where he joined a large law firm. Over the years he had been very successful and was now a senior partner. His wife came from the wealthy Protestant business class of this southern California city. Over four decades, the Cohens had one child, enjoyed a happy family life, and became well-to-do, respected members of the city's elite.

Winthrop Cohen was the son of an unsuccessful small businessman, a second-generation Jewish American who had gone from one failed business to another; his mother, a teacher and nonobservant Jew, had intentionally given him an aristocratic- and Protestant-sounding first name as a sign of her high aspirations for his success.* Winthrop's maternal grandfather, her father, had been successful as a builder of residential apartments, and Winthrop Cohen referred to himself as a "builder." "My father was a failure. He couldn't make a go of business, or family, or himself really. But I was like my grandfather. I was a builder, building a very successful career and a family. I'm proud of what I accomplished in *this* part of my life."

About his three years in the Marines, Winthrop Cohen was less proud, and he had been silent for four decades at the time I met him. Neither to family nor friends nor for purposes of advancing his legal and business interests had he spoken of his wartime experience. He purposely avoided veterans' organizations and the alumni gatherings of his Marine unit. When an article appeared in a local newspaper in the

*To me his name, with its contrast of Protestant upper class and Jewish lower middle class, and the contrast of his scars, one of which, as I've noted, looks like a scar from an elite duel and the other like a workingman's injury, highlights the man's dividedness, which helps explain what he was about. Over the years I came to think of him by his full name, Winthrop Cohen, rather than as just Winthrop. In this chapter I use his full name quite often in order to convey this sense.

1950s listing winners of military decorations in the city, it carried Winthrop's name but neither his picture nor his story; he had refused to be interviewed. When sick a decade after the war with complications of the hepatitis he had been infected with in the service, he explicitly rejected the suggestion of going to the local veterans' hospital. "I did all I could to put it all behind me. I froze it out. Even memories, whenever they popped up, I pushed them away. Until now I was successful. I was aware of course that I had a hidden life, a part of me that discredited who I was, I mean had become, but I could control it, until now."

What so thoroughly shook Winthrop Cohen were the memories of beach landings, fighting in the jungle, and, most of all, killing. "I was made over into a killer. A proficient, remorseless killer. I probably killed dozens of enemy soldiers. Most at a distance, but several very close up. One, I bashed his head in with my rifle butt after he infiltrated our lines. He was a young kid. I guess my own age. I just kept hitting him in the face with that end of the rifle. I broke everything, his nose, his mouth, his eyes. He had knifed the guy in the next hole. I heard the scream. I came running. The kid froze. I could have shot him. But I wanted to really hurt him, so I destroyed him blow after blow, till the rifle was covered in blood and gore. Then I sat down and retched. Another Jap (I hate the word now, but I used [it] plenty then)—a fat sergeant—was wounded in the gut. He had been part of a machine gun crew that tore our unit to pieces. I just shot him. But that wasn't enough. I was uncontrollable, in a rage. I took my bayonet and . . . well, better not say what I did, but it was bad. We mutilated them sometimes, and they did even worse things to our guys.

"But these two murders aren't the worst. You can understand them in a way and maybe even say things to justify
them. But I did something, something so awful, there is—
there can be no justification, no explanation, nothing to make
it seem right. Nothing can exonerate me. This is the thing I
have hidden all these years. The secret I have kept. The thing
I did that can't, can never be undone.

"He must have been a military doctor. We overran his position. A small field hospital. There were guys on stretchers,
almost dead. He raised his hands, dropping the stethoscope
at his feet. He had been bent over this stretcher, treating a guy
with a lot of blood on his chest. He raised his hands and looked
at me. His eyes were fixed on me. He just watched me. I can
see him—so quiet, just waiting. Thoughtful, sensitive. He
didn't plead. He didn't say anything. He didn't move at all.
He just looked at me. When I force myself to see it all over
again, he seems so human, so sympathetic. His face was
drawn and sad, waiting. Oh, God! I shot him. I killed him. He
slid to the ground still looking at me. And I . . . I shot him
again and again.

"At that point, let's face it, we weren't taking prisoners.
But saying that is no good. I could have taken him prisoner.
It was me, Winthrop Cohen, not we or they, who killed him.
In cold blood. Without any threat. There is no other word
for it. I murdered him. I murdered a doctor while he tended
to his wounded men. Pure and simple. I killed an innocent
man—no, I really think it is worse than that. I often think of
that doctor. Who he was. What he did. What was he thinking? He waited, but he knew, he seemed to know what I
would do. He didn't run or plead or fight. He just watched

me. I mean, in my dreams he watches me. He waits. He accepts what I do.

"The more I think about him the more Christlike he becomes, from the sorrow in his eyes to the bullet wounds and blood. I murdered a healer, a man of deep humanity. I'm sure of that.

"How could I? How could I do that?" Winthrop Cohen wept. His voice became strangled. He made no effort now to control the flow of feeling, which swept over him in great sobs.

I reached out to touch his arm. "I hear you. I understand." But in fact I didn't and couldn't understand an experience that seemed to me as gruesome as anything I had heard. We both sat there in silence, stunned by the horrible remembrance; an image of the murdered Japanese doctor took over the room. There were no words to undo what Winthrop Cohen had done or to make up for what he had gone through.

"There is no end to it, you know. No way to close it out. I can't go back and change what happened. I want to. But I can never change what I did. I don't accept the usual. . . . It's war. Men do bad things, have to do awful things. Everything pure I believe in, I betrayed. I was raised to aspire to do the right things. My mother was a humanist. She taught me to love books. She made me feel that we Jews were different, special. Because we were bound to God, we were bound to doing good in the world. And look at me. I destroyed what I was raised to value. How can I face myself?

"When we were on the troopship waiting to board the landing craft, my first time, a lot of us were scared, and try as we did to hide it, it showed. We shivered, stuttered, vomited. Wet our pants. I knew I was scared. Then some fierce Marine major turned on us. He called us every name in the book, and then he bellowed, 'Most of you shits will die on this beach. Just be sure when you're hit, you goddamn fall forward. So you don't get in the way of the guys behind you.' He meant it. His job was to take the beach and advance. You were nothing but his tools to do it. Expendable. That's what no one comprehends outside of battle. You killed and got killed. That's the way you were trained. To be tough as hell, hard, truly hard, and that means inhuman, cruelly inhuman.

"That's the other part of it. I was no aberration. I was normal, supernormal. A hero. The hero taught to kill, and along the way to betray every decent value of peacetime society. If you couldn't do it, you were mocked until you did, or thrown aside, so some other poor SOB could do it. I mock myself because I succeeded so well . . . because I can't turn back or turn it off."

Winthrop Cohen's remorse and regret were accompanied by almost all the cardinal symptoms of depression listed in the American Psychiatric Association's *Diagnostic and Statistical Manual* (which was in its third edition at that time): sadness, anhedonia (lack of pleasure), loss of sexual interest, sleep disturbance with early morning wakening, profound lack of energy, difficulty concentrating, agitation, appetite loss with a ten-pound weight loss, slowing down of all motor functions, and deep feelings of guilt, worthlessness, and hopelessness. As a young psychiatrist who had recently passed the clinical examination of the American Board of Neurology and Psychiatry, I knew that the appropriate treatment was to combine the right psychopharmacological drug with at least several months of weekly psychotherapy. That's what I recommended and what Winthrop agreed to and complied with.

Winthrop Cohen's clinical depression responded to a short course of antidepressant medication and psychodynamic psychotherapy focused on clarifying and interpreting his wartime trauma in the context of his biography and intimate relations. After eight weeks, he no longer stared off into space or looked agitated or seriously depressed. He returned to work. His wife and daughter thanked me for treating this "breakdown." But Winthrop Cohen never thanked me. To the contrary, at our last meeting, he implied that I was part of the societal collusion to cover up the threatening implications of war experiences such as his.

"I can put it away again. I don't feel the same pressure. I can sleep, and eat, and fornicate again. But you know as well as I do that what's bothering me can't be treated or cured. Job said: 'I will maintain my integrity. I will hold on to my righteousness.' I did neither. I soiled myself as I was soiled. I lost my humanity as those around me did the same. You don't have any answers. Nor do I. Save to live with it. To realize I did the worst is to understand how ordinary men do bad things. How ordinary Americans were so anti-Semitic at that time. How ordinary Germans did what they did during the Holocaust. How all of us are capable of murder. In the midst of war when all hell breaks loose and you are empowered to act with impunity, you can do horror and be decorated for it. And you can dine out for decades telling war stories, stories that are untrue. Because who can face up to the reality of the evil we did? Only the patriotic memories last. The killing is forgotten. The suffering remembered, because it is legitimate to speak of it. What can't be said—I mean in public—is what I did. What does that tell you about the soul?"

Winthrop Cohen asked me this question two decades ago. I wrote it down verbatim in my clinical notes. The commentary I added alongside Winthrop's words in my notes is not worth repeating because it seems banal and disturbingly off the mark. I must have felt my clinical prowess was threatened because I commented solely on the depression and its effect, and what happened after treatment. I knew, of course, there was a larger, more telling ethical issue, but I turned away from it.

Perhaps I was misled by Winthrop Cohen's final word. Soul, after all, turns the force of his critique to the inner self as if it were isolated from the world. But everything else he said points to the world. What does that tell you about the world? It is just as damning and sounds in retrospect the right conclusion. Job referred to his inner state with the Hebrew term *ka'as*, "vexed." That is the same meaning Chinese victims of the Cultural Revolution gave to their feeling state, which they named with the term *fan zao*—vexed in the sense of being shaken by an outer force that powerfully agitates our inner state. It reminds me of the inseparable tie between our selves and our local worlds, emotion and value. And it reminds me of Winthrop Cohen, because he had been shaken by the brutal force of war and what he felt was a just response to what he had done and what had been done to him.

Eight years ago I learned from a former colleague that Winthrop Cohen had died of liver failure, the long-term consequence of the hepatitis he had contracted in the Pacific war. I went back to my clinical notes, something I do not routinely do, because I was troubled by something unfinished, ethical questions I had never addressed. I tried to rethink the case in the much wider context of twentieth-century American society. What had mattered to Winthrop Cohen was to move ahead, to succeed at a high level. His mother had set him on the course of moving from the Jewish lower middle class, to which their prospects had fallen, to the Protestant elite class that then dominated American society. She did it with the name she gave to him, the stories she told him, and the high expectation she held for him. The negative example of his father's repeated failures was masked by the positive example of his grandfather's achievement.

But Winthrop Cohen also embodied a religious ideal. He bore the mark of a people that defined itself, in his words, as special in its relation to God, in its historical sense of the elevated demands of its ethical culture, and in its stubborn struggles to square religious values with real-life problems through especially strong concern with suffering, healing, and medicine. In the radically changed ethos of battle, Winthrop Cohen had succeeded brilliantly as a warrior—a success that would be matched by his secular career, which advanced from one achievement to another. But as a human being, he had failed in his own mind in the most existential way. He had killed, and not just with professional competence but with savage explosions of rage. And he had killed someone who, he said to me, even at the moment of being killed practiced the very ethical values Winthrop Cohen associated with his own religion. He called this military doctor "innocent," "a healer." Of course we don't really know if this was so. For all we, and Winthrop, know, the Japanese medic may have participated in atrocities too. If he personally hadn't done so, other Japanese had. And of all America's wars, the war Winthrop fought in seems to come closest to the justifications of a just war. Even if we find this rationalization unappealing, Winthrop Cohen was fighting for his life. In the chaotic hell of battle he had done what he had to do, I thought, trying even in my interpretive strategy to protect this vulnerable former soldier who refused all artifice and counterargument. Wasn't his implacable self-criticism a vindication of his decency? But for Winthrop it was the existential reality of his moral imagination that counted. He had done what he could never accept. He had done more than betray his ideals; he had done something so evil there was no atonement, only punishment. He, a Jew on his way to success in the Christian world, had killed a "Christlike" figure. He said that. And my thoughts now completed the charge: he had thereby enacted a vicious myth that has been immensely destructive over so many generations. His personal tragedy, I now told myself, was deepened by the embodiment of this terribly dangerous collective myth.

For Winthrop Cohen, what mattered most at the moment of his heroism and horror was killing and avoiding being killed. He proved to others and himself that he could do it. He remembered, however, and he remembered with a vengeance. Even forty years after the event, he could put himself right back into the fighting. His memory had the purpose of taking vengeance on himself. He could not forget or forgive himself. He had justice in mind. And so we have the telling, and not uncommon, paradox of a man with mental illness (depression) giving voice to powerfully disturbing insights about the danger of ordinary life and the burden of moral responsibility that a normal man could neither think nor speak.

I wrote in the introduction that this is a book about ordinary people caught up in ordinary *and* extraordinary experiences that define the dangers and uncertainties of actual moral life. Twelve million Americans were in military service in the Second World War. Only several million bore arms, and fewer still were combat troops. Even so, Winthrop Cohen's experience of war was shared by many, many servicemen. Not necessarily the atrocities, but surely the killing and being killed are what combat was about. In this sense it was and still is the ordinary moral experience of war. We have no idea how many former soldiers came to interrogate that life, but the novels, poems, and works of criticism in the postwar years indicate that some did. Perhaps this is what makes Winthrop Cohen at least somewhat extraordinary: his later life was obsessed by questions of wartime guilt for actions he committed that increasingly seemed to him inhuman and ethically indefensible.

Extraordinary experiences—the end of life, emergencies, extreme social conditions—concentrate the focus of ordinary men and women on what is most at stake for them and for those around them. Just so, Winthrop Cohen came to see what mattered most in warfare for him and for others. Proving himself a warrior among warriors; channeling his fear and rage into deadly acts that destroyed the enemy, even conspicuously so; doing all in his power to protect himself and the small band of servicemen with whom he had bonded in a tight fighting unit—all were commonsense commitments and actions that he was trained to perform and did indeed carry out, participating in a shared moral world. This held true until that moment when he saw himself step beyond what he could personally countenance even in the heat of battle. Then he began to question that moral world: its sources, its taken-for-granted commitments to do what it takes to succeed, and its consequences. Where did his moral responsibility lie? What were the limits to what he (and by implication others) could and would do? When was his moral imagination meant to clarify boundaries and protect against going too far? How could he deal with acts of atrocity when the extreme conditions had changed and he returned home once more to another local world, where radically different things mattered most and where the actions he participated in ran directly contrary to what was approved and valued?

I THOUGHT ONCE AGAIN about Winthrop Cohen in 2004 as I read of the atrocities committed by American soldiers and marines in Iraq. And once again I felt haunted by his refusal to hide behind conventional justifications that shift responsibility from the perpetrator to leaders and on to society as a whole. No wonder we want (need) to forget what moral experience, especially under extreme conditions like war, is really about. To understand how our world can change so radically that many of the things most at stake for us are altered fundamentally—such as life becoming cheap, decency and honor abandoned, anything becoming permissible in a gray zone that tolerates cunning and brute force on behalf of survival—can be a disorienting experience. Such a troubling experience can alienate and depress us. We become alienated by the value gap before and after change, by the stark disparity between words and deeds, and by how once taken-for-granted local values begin to look when we better understand what stands behind them, what they really mean. And we can become depressed when we realize that we are so dependent on local values at a particular time and place that we are vulnerable, to a degree not previously appreciated, to the danger of influence and to our own readily misplaced loyalty. We also learn that it is not just dangerous local values that put us at risk. Our own failures in imagining alternative realities, carrying through with moral responsibilities, and preventing vengeful overreaction greatly compound the dangers we face.

To challenge local common sense and to go even further and question our own sensibility puts us at odds with the way the world is. It also has the potential to undermine our sense of self and seriously upset our emotional stability. This is what happened to Winthrop Cohen. He had first tried to forget what had taken place in his moral life. But over forty years he had come to critique his world and himself in the most basic terms. He became outraged by the disparity in truth between what we say we value at times when we are under no serious threat and what we actually are capable of doing when we feel what really matters could be taken from us. He thought of this divide as hypocrisy. It might make life more livable, but it also promoted actions that were frankly inhuman and unethical. Viewed in this perspective, ordinary life looked deeply troubling because it disguised the cunning and connivance that made survival, security, and stability possible. Winthrop alleged these things and more, in words both direct and metaphoric.

Memories can (and do) kill, when they foster acts of revenge. The words are in my psychotherapy notes, but I seemed to have missed almost completely their ethical resonance, so fixated was I on treating the depressive symptoms and what

I then took to be their underlying cause in Winthrop Cohen's psychopathology. As Winthrop's symptoms improved, he was not focused on depression. He was bothered by a deeper concern that I suppose I was then unprepared to name and address. Moral experience, he implied, can lead a normal person toward murder. Normality, not pathology, was the problem. Normality could be abusive; it was dangerous.

The atrocities at the American military prison at Abu Ghraib in Iraq occurred in a local world that condoned and encouraged the humiliation of prisoners, assault on their cultural values, and the abuse of deadly force. Atrocities were perpetrated in the name of intelligence gathering. This sad state of affairs became, among the group of military police guards, normal. Justification of a general kind was provided by military higher-ups. They wanted information on the growing Iraqi insurgency and on specific terrorist threats to the United States. The alleged abuses—threatening young prisoners with attack dogs who on occasion were allowed to bite, forcing prisoners in groups into sexual positions, and perhaps even beating several prisoners to death—went one or more steps beyond what was prescribed in the military manual. But were these practices, especially the nonlethal ones, that far outside the ballpark of police actions aimed at softening up prisoners for interrogation? The attacks of 9/11, the war on terrorism, and fighting the increasingly deadly insurgency in Iraq were the reasons given by Pentagon and other Bush administration officials for aggressive interrogations. Backed by these official justifications, and with growing feelings of fear and revenge in response to attacks by insurgents and riots by prisoners, prison guards participated in a moral milieu that created abuse as a routine. The moral scenario I have described of actual dangers leading to overresponses that escalate danger actually took place. I don't mean to exculpate the abusive guards. Their individual actions were unacceptable. They were responsible for the abuses. They went well beyond acceptable rules of engagement and ethical limits, and did so, at least in several cases, for their own sadistic pleasure. There is a difference between their actions and what Winthrop Cohen did in a life-threatening combat situation. And yet Winthrop warned that further abuses would happen, had to happen, because of the moral conditions established by war. When I reread my notes and rediscovered Winthrop Cohen's voice of ethical alarm mixed in with my technical psychiatric observations, I was appalled at my own failure to acknowledge the value crisis and human tragedy that he had insisted were the heart of the matter. How had I been so far off the mark?

My notes speculated about dissociation—the splitting of cognition from affect, action from moral sensibility—which was coming back as a fad in psychiatry just then. The basic argument was that in situations of extreme threat, we separate thought from feeling so that we can flee, fight, or, if we become victims, block out the brutal reality of assault, freezing it in a cut-off traumatic space outside of consciousness and memory. It all seemed to fall into place. People are able to repress traumatic memories for a certain amount of time. Eventually the memories resurface and cause anxiety, depression, and other mental problems. Trauma, once split off into dissociated states, the theory stated, reemerges as post-traumatic stress disorder or other conditions. My original analysis of Winthrop's problem is an example of the seduction of the professional by the analytic framework he is trained to apply. Allan Young, a leading medical anthropologist of trauma, calls this seduction "the harmony of illusions." By this Young means that the therapist applies an interpretive frame of traumatic memories causing symptoms, a frame that comes to shape the therapist's understanding of the patient's post-traumatic experience. Once the condition is described in terms of repressed or dissociated trauma, the refigured experience comes to seem a confirmation of the theory. In fact, it is all a huge tautology. That's where I was, caught in a professional loop that left me deaf to Winthrop Cohen's complaint: what was at stake for him was the soul and not the trauma, the moral crisis and not the Oedipal conflict.

I'm certain Winthrop meant to leave me with a discomforting feeling. He wanted me to feel what he felt: namely, that what he was suffering was not disease but tragedy. He could not come to terms with the morality or normality of his actions during the war, and he knew I couldn't either. He had been remade in a terrifying and devastating way, and yet those very qualities later in life spurred him toward critical self-reflection. As I have learned in research from those who have suffered other forms of political violence, being vexed shakes one out of comforting illusions and can be contagious. It undermines confidence in justice and goodness while pressing one to create both in one's life. It doesn't necessarily respond to treatment. In place of healing it gives voice to pain and suffering about the sometimes defeating reality of our lives: a seemingly despairing reality that, when we confront it, can only be lived through, we imagine, enduring the unmasterable. It is exactly here where religion, ethics, and aesthetics remake meaning, creating hope. And seen in this way, there is something uplifting about Winthrop Cohen's ethical framing of his life and times. There is hope in his moral courage, his grim fidelity to a damning reflection on self and world. There is hope in his implacable commitment to an unblinded acknowledgment of having participated in evil. There is hope in his refusal to abandon a language of remorse and regret, and in his lived commitment to the impossibility and yet the unavoidability of repentance. And amidst great danger and huge uncertainty, hope is what makes the human condition livable.

3

Idi Bosquet-Remarque

T all, thin but muscular, her pale skin freckled by the sun, her brown-blond hair pulled back into a severe ponytail setting off large, soft gray-green eyes, Ida Hélène Bosquet-Remarque, known as Idi, was a French American woman who for over fifteen years, from 1980 to the late 1990s, worked as a field representative for several different international aid agencies and, later, European foundations, first and only briefly in Southeast Asia and subsequently in sub-Saharan Africa. Idi was an expert in working with refugee and internally displaced women and children, and with the local bureaucrats, police, soldiers, religionists, and health and social welfare professionals who surround them. I narrate her story because Idi was a friend of two decades who represents for me our finest impulse to acknowledge the suffering of others and to devote our lives and careers to making a difference (practically and ethically) in their lives, even if that difference must

be limited and transient. I tell her story because of her remarkable moral responsibility for those in deep poverty and
desperate difficulties, and because of her willingness to do
good in the world almost anonymously, without seeking career advancement or public attention.

Her focus was humanitarian assistance. She worked in war
zones, failed states, politically unstable border zones, and
places afflicted with other, less clearly identifiable forms of
political violence, such as structural violence in which the
policies of the state and the global powers place the poorest
at great risk for premature death from malnutrition, expo-
sure to toxins, transmission of highly infectious diseases, and
other sources of health inequality. Although she held an advanced degree in sociology from the Sorbonne and another
in international public policy from the University of London,
Idi managed to eschew managerial or policy-level positions
in the central headquarters or regional offices of the NGOs
that have employed her.

Idi's work took place in Africa at a time when that continent's
societies were undergoing tumultuous change. Under the oppressive regime of structural adjustment policies insisted upon
by the World Bank and International Monetary Fund as their
requirement for poor countries to receive economic assistance,
those recipient countries during the 1970s and 1980s were forced
to severely cut public spending for health services, social welfare, and education. These policies placed tremendous pressure on the poorest peasants and urban dwellers, while
addicting their countries' leaders to repeated cycles of heavy
borrowing, near bankruptcy, retraction of the public sector,
further debt, and further borrowing. The result, abetted by

endemic corruption among the elite classes, was greater and greater debt that weakened nation after nation. So when instances of sectarian and ethnic strife occurred, there was little to hold societies together. The upshot was failing and failed states, states that could not provide for vulnerable citizens or carry out basic services. It was in this postcolonial context that ethnic and regional conflict began to tear apart Liberia, Sierra Leone, Congo, Rwanda, Somalia, Sudan, Angola, Mozambique, Côte d'Ivoire, and others. The Rwandan genocide, the repeated famines in the Horn of Africa, and the splintering of the Congo were only the most extreme examples of breakdown. There were, of course, relative success stories, such as postapartheid South Africa. But even among the more successful countries, during this period epidemics of AIDS, tuberculosis, and malaria spread out of control. Into this chaotic situation, nongovernmental organizations (NGOs) such as Oxfam, Save the Children, Doctors Without Borders, and hundreds of others brought humanitarian assistance from international donors. Especially active were international governmental organizations such as UNICEF; governmental organizations such as the Scandinavian, Canadian, and British aid agencies; American foundations, including Ford, Rockefeller, and Carnegie; and religious-based humanitarian assistance and medical relief programs. In this swirl of activity, some programs were truly effective, but many, many failed owing to corruption, mismanagement, cultural barriers, and a dismaying combination of donor politics and local politics. It became characteristic for programs to end after running for only a few years as new projects captured the increasingly short attention span of the global donor community, before old ones had any chance of being evaluated or generalized. Still, many humanitarian assistance workers stayed on under dire circumstances and responded to crisis after crisis—famine, civil war, epidemics of newly emergent deadly infectious diseases such as Ebola and AIDS, mass migration of populations out of war zones, trafficking in women and drugs, destruction of environments and animal populations, and on and on. Idi was one of the thousands of foreign experts who worked with NGOs in Africa to aid populations in crisis, respond to emergencies, and deal with the deep structural inequalities that placed vulnerable people at great risk. Her skill was in working closely with local people, doing what she called "field work."

"You know what I mean, our equivalent of ethnography [the research method of social and cultural anthropologists]. Mucking around in villages and market towns; learning the local dialect; living closer to how our clients do, or just a level better than they do, to be honest. Identifying the most vulnerable and struggling to organize supplies, infrastructure, and support. Building latrines, protecting drinking water, putting up tents, vaccinating infants and children. That's what we do as well as triage medical cases—when there is someplace to triage them to. We also need to locate and recruit part-time staff. Identify local people who can help out. Keep the police and army calm. You name it, we do it. . . . Water. Now, that's as big as food. Burials. Death is everywhere under these conditions. But then so are births. I could go on. I get an awfully good feeling out of getting things done under truly difficult conditions when they have a human effect. Stay put for a few years, then move on somewhere else. . . . Another list of problems, another community to learn, another order of possibilities. Friends, good friends to make and work with."

I had known Idi since her college days in the mid-1970s. I was a research fellow at Harvard and in the process of moving to the University of Washington, where I would go on to build a program in medical anthropology and cultural psychiatry until I returned to Harvard in 1982. Idi was a student at an elite private liberal arts college in Massachusetts. She had heard of my research and asked me to be an informal advisor for her field research and senior honors thesis, something I have done often over the years. Over two decades I got to know her quite well, and whenever she returned to the United States she stopped in to see me.

Idi had a nearly lifelong commitment to working with people in poverty and in extreme conditions. Her senior honors thesis was a remarkably mature analysis of ethnographies, that is, firsthand descriptions of villages, neighborhoods, and networks by anthropologists who had learned the local language, lived for one or more years observing local affairs, and participated in family life, work, and religious and political activities. Idi's thesis centered on ethnographies of the poor and marginal in the world's poorest societies. Most striking was the interest she devoted to the ethical implications of anthropological research among the disadvantaged. She bravely concluded, much against the prevailing wisdom of the time, that it was ethically unacceptable to study those in distress without first providing practical assistance to alleviate their suffering. At the time, many ethnographers had as their goal "scientific description," which put into practice an ideal of formal and usually distant relations to informants as well as formal methods of gathering and analyzing data. They believed that if you intervened in the life of your research subjects, it would bias the findings. So the idea, strange as it may sound today, was to avoid being involved in practical applications such as health care and social service for the local community. She was equally suspicious of "witnessing" as an end in itself. She didn't believe that simply recording voices of sufferers and analyzing their stories of distress could be an end in itself. You had to act, she insisted, to help people. And she was not alone in her beliefs; she pointed out that the great existentialist French writer Albert Camus similarly believed that engagement—that is, being personally committed to others and taking on real responsibility for joining them in resolving major problems in the messiness of local life— was as much about practical action as it was about empathy and solidarity. Idi was also somewhat suspicious of advocacy in research unless it translated solid findings into direct action. Here, Idi was criticizing social scientists who spoke on behalf of indigenous people but who either had not carried out systematic research, or, if they had, did not base their comments on new findings. She feared they would usurp the right of local people to represent themselves, while adding nothing new to the analysis of what needed to be done.

Her thesis was based on a half year's research in an East African setting, which gave her ample experience to develop an informed opinion about each of these issues. I remember almost exactly a conversation I had with her, shortly after she returned from her thesis research, about professional burn-out. Idi remarked mordantly, to my initial surprise, that journalists and even social scientists were placing too much

emphasis on the suffering of the expatriate staff of humanitarian organizations. Because they spoke English, were ur-
bane, and could connect quickly with foreign visitors, their
stories got told. For example, news reports about southern
Sudan's periodic famines often centered on the foreign experts themselves. They are asked what it's like to work in
such a place and how they can do their work under such
"primitive" conditions. Harassed African mothers, holding
dying children in their arms, whom they are trying to feed,
only form the background. They are rendered silent by the
foreign interviewers. The desperate mothers are good for a
word or two, but otherwise they are left outside the conversation that goes on with the expatriate aid workers. To Idi's
mind this led to an undervaluing of the suffering of the people
the foreign staff were there to assist. Idi belabored this point in
a manner that seemed to me atypical for her. She criticized the
Europeans and Americans with whom she worked for their
tendency to live in their own world. They were protected from
the conditions (the filth, the flies, the hovels) of the refugees
and internally displaced. They did not have to share those
slightly better but still grindingly poor conditions (offices without glass in the windows, torn clothes, broken chairs and desks,
an absence of writing or toilet paper) that made the lives of
their local professional colleagues (African doctors, dentists,
ministers, teachers) so difficult. Idi targeted what I knew to be
real issues, but her tone was, for a young woman who was
characterologically sympathetic, uncharacteristically strident
and unsympathetic. This was a matter that really bothered her.

   This critique was prelude to an even more troubling concern, one that Idi could see directly affected herself. Foreign

aid workers and their affiliate NGOs received funding and recognition for projects that they themselves initiated and controlled. But didn't this setup, Idi wondered, contribute to the problems of poverty and community inefficacy? Shouldn't it be local workers, not foreigners, who took charge and held the principal responsibility for the failure or success of a project? Shouldn't it be those local workers who therefore received the credit? Because if local people running local projects got the credit, then those projects might be much more likely to be sustained.

Since the aid workers were mainly whites from rich countries, there was among them a certain smell of neocolonialism, as well as self-serving careerism, by which she meant not only as a professional but also, she put it mercilessly, as a "saint." Hence for Idi there was a problem she referred to, mockingly, as "the last white hope." Perhaps this is the postcolonial equivalent of the "white man's burden" of the colonial era. For Idi, it referred to the not-so-hidden racism by which Euro-Americans saw themselves as Africa's only hope. Any successful program, it was expected, had to be led by white people, preferably heroic figures such as Albert Schweitzer. The humanitarian worker as hero, whether it was the product of the imagination of aid workers or of their Western audience, made her suspicious.

And yet Idi also could see that without foreign workers there might be no program at all—not because of some fault of local workers (though she admitted they needed to raise their level of professionalism) but because they could not command the financial and symbolic resources required to fund a program with economic, social, and political capital. The irony of her thesis, Idi remarked lightly but tellingly, was that she had found an argument against hiring someone like her. Her first real field experience had, much as she relished the work, undone her future, Idi lightly laughed.

I once had the opportunity in 1989 to observe Idi in her professional capacity in an East African country known at the time for its corrupt bureaucracy and its dismal results from numerous assistance programs. There I watched her put into practice much of what she had previously written about. She was also, under these trying circumstances (scarce funds, limited staff, political problems from organizing assistance for poor women in a marginalized and illegal squatter settlement), rather impressively effective—meaning she did more than just survive against the odds and actually had organized a serious program, small but with clear evidence of some success. The program provided food aid, clean water, latrines, low-level health services, and protection to migrant women and their children. I spoke with several of the desperate people she assisted as well as with her local colleagues, and came away, after an admittedly brief evaluation, feeling that Idi had done something unusual.

I remember one terribly thin African woman with whom I spoke about Idi. She told me she was thirty-five, yet she looked much, much older, with streaks of gray in her black hair. Her face was lined with two rows of tribal initiation scars on each cheek. She wore a colorful green dress with a yellow ribbon around her neck. She had several small children, who, despite their tattered clothes, looked reasonably healthy and laughed loudly while they ran around outside the wood frame building they shared with other families near a pit latrine and protected water source. This woman said that she owed her family members' lives and her own to Idi. She wept when she recalled: "We arrived with nothing, and people here tried to take advantage of us. This program saved us. And this program is Idi. We feel like she is one of us. She's not like the other officials. They are cold and distant." I was so taken by the obvious heartfeltness of her expression I wrote it down and included it in a letter praising Idi's efforts to a senior figure in the organization Idi worked for at the time.

Idi and I walked around a shantytown housing thousands of migrants. They illegally occupied the land and put up shacks of cardboard, cast-off metal, and sticks. The government had decided on a political strategy of ignorance. These people simply did not exist in any official way. So they required neither piped water nor sewage disposal. Children played in the dirt streets, which were slick with raw sewage and littered with broken bottles. Idi told me that when it rained the streets became streams of mud and fecal matter—a place of such contamination that recurrent diarrheal disease and skin ulcers were omnipresent. The infant mortality rate was five to ten times that of a nearby middle-class neighborhood. Standing around on the corners of dirt tracks with enormous potholes, men and a few women with dazed expressions held jars of home-distilled spirits. Alcoholism, Idi demonstrated with specific family examples, worsened the grinding of economic wretchedness. Intoxication intensified domestic violence, which in turn, Idi posited, led to depression, spasms of rage, agitation, and suicide.

"Hopelessness," she explained as I furiously scribbled notes, "is endemic here. What we are doing is helping the

more active, effective women to organize community programs to protect them and their kids, and to try to rehabili-
tate the men." We visited one family in a jerrybuilt shack. The
young wife and mother held an infant she was feeding, while
two older children played on the dirt floor. So poorly venti-
lated was the shack that I had trouble breathing. The stench
of rotting food, garbage, and feces was strong, the heat fero-
cious. Flies covered the walls. The children had thick green-
ish mucus running from their nostrils, and one had a deep,
rasping, productive cough. Idi spoke to the young mother in
Kiswahili. She told her about the community clinic where
public health nurses supported by Idi's organization could
treat the children without charge. The woman looked exhausted. Her husband was in the hospital with tuberculosis.
She had no family or friends nearby to help her. She explained
to Idi shyly that because she was desperate she sold herself
for sex to various of the men who stood drunk or drugged
near the shack. Idi cautioned her about STDs and HIV/AIDS,
but it was clear the woman already knew about the risk. She
simply could not demand safe sex from customers who refused to wear condoms. Idi was already organizing local
nurses to develop a more substantial AIDS prevention project.
She tried to enlist this woman, but the woman prevaricated.
Idi later told me that there was a stigma associated with AIDS
that spread from infected people to local AIDS programs, and
as a result, her clients were reluctant to join.

After we left the shack, Idi remarked that this program was
one of several new ones she was initiating. Idi seemed very
tired. She turned to me and whispered that it was when she
saw what terribly poor young women like this one were up

against that she began to despair whether it was possible to do anything useful.

I asked Idi how she did it. How could she find the stamina, perseverance, and commitment to respond to such overwhelming conditions? How in the midst of global epidemics of substance abuse, related violence, HIV/AIDS and other diseases, and structural inequality could she succeed?

She responded with a twinkle in her eyes and a sly smile: "Don't go and overestimate our success. Just keeping clients alive and staff going is a kind of success. But how do we do it? What's the alternative? Give up? Shut down? Run away? Once you rule those things out, you do the one thing left to do. . . . I focus on what needs to get done. Which in this case means not everything these poor women need, but at least a few of the more crucial things that help them survive and fight on. Which amounts to as much as the damn officials will let drop through their grasping fingers. Look at the district officer [a local government administrator] here. He isn't a bad guy at all, but he can't even record the displaced because then it would commit the government to actually offer real services. He's been told the government won't do that, hence he proceeds as if the migrants and refugees don't exist. As I said, he's not a bad fellow. He is intelligent, has a degree from an American university, knows the kinds of things he should be doing, but he is administratively bound. He can't act. And if he did on his own cross the higher-ups, they'd never let him have the resources. Worse still, he's told to be a gatekeeper to the state's resources. And hey, he has to live too—poor soul. His salary is completely inadequate, so he is going to look for ways to put some public money aside for private purposes. He's got to, for his wife and kids. He really would like to do something, but he can't afford to. I call that a plus. He's a potential ally. He just doesn't know it. I've worked with much worse. . . . I give him and those who aren't as enlightened and well-meaning as he is the strong impression that I'm going to get these people who are sick, starving, scared, living on the street and in the shacks at least some of the things they need. . . . 'Don't lecture me about the regulations, which I already know and you know I know. Don't hide behind politically correct talk. . . . For God's sake, listen to these poor people; these women know what they need; they may just have the answers. You know it's not as difficult as you make it seem; even under these pitiful conditions, you can do good. I can be easy to work with. I won't be in your face. No threat. No problem. Hey, you can take the credit. You might even come out looking like a winner. If this program is going to succeed, if these desperate people are going to succeed, you need to get something out of it too. I won't stop you. But don't, just don't avoid me. Don't brush me off. I can help you, but if necessary I can bring you trouble too. So friend, let's get it done!'"

Tough words spoken with a hardheaded realization of the art of what is feasible. But the voice was soft and also carried with it the hope of what is possible. The professional expertise and personal conviction, both formidable, were carried so lightly and with such good humor that the message was not an unattractive one.

Idi didn't exclude herself from the searchlight of criticism. "You know, out here I feel I have at one moment or other made every mistake. Yet in the end things work out. Oh, not everything, but more than you might imagine. More often I'm the problem, or my program is. I've even wondered paradoxically if you need to be a 'problem' to accomplish anything substantial. If we don't break the business-as-usual routine, we don't get the attention of the power holders, and without their attention little can happen. But I'm not here to be a culture broker. It's too late for that kind of mediation between local and outside interests. We need to act. So I act as if I were a local player. Of course I'm not. But if I pretend to be one, I sometimes can make things happen. Of course not always for the best. And when you act like a local you had better be prepared for the same rough treatment these women experience. I've had that happen too. What I mean is that you need to act locally but keep some of the clout of an outsider. I never get the balance exactly right. And I've blundered badly with real consequences. But if you don't risk it you become like so many of my peers, a stock player who can be manipulated. On the other hand, when I fall off the balance beam, which I do from time to time, there is a big noise and a big mess. I did that with a needle exchange program that was, ah, a little ahead of its time and without the proper license, a program to protect battered wives that was, well, licensed but perhaps a little excessive in hiding women from their husbands." Idi had learned from these and other misadventures that negotiating with the local political leaders was crucial.

To be effective she fashioned a simple strategy: she often traveled with an entourage of migrants and locals who saw her as their spokesperson when dealing with the administrative apparatus of the state. Because of their support, state officials could not dismiss her as a foreigner meddling in things she didn't understand. The cachet (communication channels and cash) of the institutions Idi represented gave her the means to make things happen, including at higher levels of the local political economic system. In one instance I observed, this combination of local voices and external power created assistance for several displaced families who were homeless, with the promise of more to come for a larger group of women and children. In that case, Idi threatened a visiting social welfare official who worked in the ministry that if he didn't participate in a meeting in the slum, which he had told her was impossible for him to do because his ministry did not recognize the existence of the slum, she would bring together the foreign representatives of the major NGOs and take them to see his boss. In such a meeting, she promised, she would criticize him so that his job would be in jeopardy. But once this official met with her clients, Idi stepped back and let them raise specific demands for better housing and financial assistance for their children. She had rehearsed these women; now she stood behind them. Once the meeting ended, she went out of her way to be supportive and nice to the ministry official. Nonetheless, Idi recognized that her affiliation with a small European NGO and her lack of wide recognition restricted her work and limited her successes.

"I don't delude myself. I'm not the UN High Commissioner [for Refugees]. I'm not even the major local coordinator. I know I represent a relatively small organization with just a few programs of limited scale. At first it imposed a terrible sense of restriction that made me uneasy. How can I justify helping only a few? But now, years into it, I feel more at ease. It's a more human scale. We know our clients. Invest in them.

Follow them up. They mean something to us as real people. They are never just a number. I feel like nothing is perfect in the world. You do what you can with what you have. Would I like to do more? Of course. Can I live with the limits? Yes, I can. Well, not when I see so many desperate faces. But yes, definitely yes, when I work with those people I can help. My policy training tells me I got it all wrong. But my lived experience in this place tells me I'm doing okay."

The more I spoke to Idi the more she had to say about this tension between what was good from a programmatic perspective and what was good from her own more complexly human, on-the-ground experience.

"When I was a student it [the plans and strategies for running a successful program] seemed clearer. Now things are gray most of the time. The more I get to know the people we assist the more complex they are. Few are simply victims. Some were also perpetrators . . . even in the same family. . . . You hear stories of betrayal. How often am I told not to trust or believe others. It can get awfully confused and paranoid. Corruption is an instance too. When I started out I could smell it like rot. Now I don't recognize the odor so easily. Is the poor DO [district officer] corrupt because he tries to make financial gain out of our programs so that his family can eat better? After all, the government assumes he can't live on his salary, which is meager, and that he will supplement 'creatively.' If the sums are small, and it's not outright theft, I tend not to get in a huff. It's when you see the higher-ups squeeze and grind people to live like the proverbial fat cats that I get really upset and blow the whistle. I have only the greatest disdain for those robbers. Their greed is so destructive. Otherwise I have come to accept we all need to muddle through somehow, and muddling can be a very thin space from corruption."

Idi reserved her most devastating criticisms for the higher-ups in several of the NGOs and international governmental agencies with whom she has worked. "They can't keep their hands off micromanaging what we do in the field. They often have little sense of what our on-the-ground problems are about. They have usually formed their policy decisions even before they talk with us and see the programs. They are uncomfortable in the extreme with our clients. Maybe they fear catching some infectious disease. I know I sound satiric, but believe me, that's how some of them really are. In New York, London, and Paris they dream up new objectives, rewrite our charge, spend money on nonsense. Every year we've got to have a new theme to catch the attention of the media. New buzzwords. Everything is spun by these guys to make public relations pizzazz. I think they test them on politically correct speech: how else to explain their sterilized jargon? I've had a couple try to mess with my programs. It made me very cynical very fast. And cynicism is the kiss of death in this business. Better to move on to some other posting than to wallow in cynicism. I watched too many good people end up that way. I'm no romantic—you know that—but you've got to keep some kind of vision of what genuinely ought to be if you're going to work in this profession. You don't have to buy all the human rights talk, so much is flummery. But you do have to commit yourself to helping people in distress. And that requires some kind of belief in the prospect of a different kind of world."

Idi enunciated these words with a light laugh and soft play of irony in her lively features, as if to undermine too definitive a critique of the humanitarian assistance community. She had come to be uncomfortable with taking too definitive a stand on her field because she had increasingly come to see it in the more complexly human terms of real individuals struggling to save highly particular programs that are a mix of successes and failures. Still, the foundational commitment in her life to the desperately poor came across with passion.

Idi was well read on the issue of women and development. She could cite facts and figures on women's lives in the developing world in regard to female infanticide, sexual abuse, genital mutilation, slavery, violence and trauma, abandonment to poverty, lack of health equity, and witchcraft accusations. The effects of patriarchy were starkly visible in her workaday world. Nonetheless, she was well balanced in discussing the subject. Most of the officials and technical experts with whom she worked were men, even though women were becoming more prominent. With these male colleagues her easy elegance was visibly attractive, and Idi was not unaware how useful this could be in her professional work. Her personal life was private, off-limits to those who were not good friends. She did this to protect herself and maintain clout within a man's world. It provided her, she told me, with a certain mystery and charisma, which was crucial in her work. She had had several close male friends, one of whom was a European journalist and another a South Asian artist. Idi never expressed an interest in marriage or children. She had perhaps a dozen close female friends whom she referred to as her "international love and support network." She often stayed with members of this "ILSN," as she called it, when she took leave time abroad.

Two were well-educated African women. They had become her closest friends.

Idi spoke with great fondness of her own family: a French American father who was an international investment banker, a French mother from a wealthy family in Burgundy who was a medical researcher in Switzerland. A younger sister was a physician with an international NGO in the Middle East, and a much younger brother was studying music at a French university. "My father's parents were poor. They immigrated to America after the war in 1946. They had family in New York state. There was also a political problem. My grandfather wasn't exactly an official of the Pétain government, but he had done something; he was a collaborator, maybe not a real war criminal, but from what I can figure out, something pretty close to that. Anyhow, they had to leave."

An East African colleague, himself a successful leader of small community projects, who knew Idi and respected her, despite often being hard on foreign experts in Africa, confided: "Idi is special. You don't see many like her. She fits in locally. Or at least tries to. She lives, more or less, on the local economy. Doesn't stay in fancy accommodations. She has lots of friends among the people she works with. She doesn't hang out after hours with expats. In fact, her best friends are two African women. Speaks Kiswahili, not fluently or even very well, but bravely. She uses it. Listens and speaks with it. People really appreciate that. As a result, she learns a lot that other representatives of international NGOs just don't get. Of course she is like a lot of people in humanitarian work: thoughtful and sympathetic. Idi, however, is also incredibly astute politically and culturally. And best of all she is calm, selfless, and just very positive. Africa is not a basket case to her; Africans are not ignorant or incapable. She knows colonial history and postcolonial theory, better than I do. But like everything else she travels light. No posturing. She also possesses a kind of natural touch for collaborating with all kinds of people and interests in order to [make] really bad situations less dangerous for women and children, to protect them."

And that's how I saw Idi too. She had made an irrevocable commitment to live among the poorest Africans as a friend and fellow member of the community, and to do all she could to help them. She was motivated by a passion for social justice and by an unwillingness to accept things as they are, which would have condemned these people to the most miserable social disparities. There were deep roots to this extraordinarily difficult but inspiring commitment. She kept alive the image of her grandfather's collaborationist past and worked against it. Everything she associated with him—collaboration with evil, racism, failure of moral vision and responsibility—she sought to reverse in her own life. She drew on her family's Catholicism, and especially liberation theology, for the priority it gave to the suffering of the poor as the grounds for social justice and personal salvation. She had read, in the original French editions, the writings of the Parisian ethical theorist and Jewish theologian Emmanuel Lévinas. His ideas became her ideas: namely, that ethics precedes everything else; that ethics itself requires face-to-face relations; that suffering is useful only in the response of the other person to the person in pain, making empathy the central ethical act. Absent this ethical response to local people and their problems, policies and programs were untethered to real lives and actual worlds.

They would be unlikely to succeed either in human terms or as practical projects. Idi persisted in her work. She stayed when other foreign aid experts departed. She connected with people at a human level deeper than program protocols.

It was because of the stability of this picture of Idi Bosquet-Remarque over so many years that I grew so concerned at our last meeting in 1997. Idi telephoned from the airport in Geneva, Switzerland, to tell me she was on her way to Boston to see friends and wanted to see me as well. This time, she said she needed my clinical advice. Those words surprised me, because she had never before made such a request. We met in my office at Harvard for several hours, then had lunch together, and afterward walked slowly around Harvard Yard, back and forth on a chilly gray fall day with the trees in splendid colors, before returning to my office.

Idi all of a sudden seemed a disturbingly different person. The twenty-two months in West and Central African war zones had taken an enormous toll. Both zones of violence were chaotic, shifting from week to week with different groups fighting for unclear and changing reasons. Civilians were the targets of brutal and deadly attacks. As a result, large groups were in movement, attempting to escape the widespread destruction. Idi had been assisting these uprooted groups of hungry, frightened, and sick families.

Idi's face was thinner and, most notably, her facial expression had changed. Gone were the lively expression and ironic smiles. Her face now looked immobile, the muscles taut, her gaze fixed in an expression of grim seriousness and hyperalert focus. While Idi spoke, her eyes looked directly into mine, her own unblinking. The contrast between their soft warmth and the hardness of her expression was striking. That contrast radiated a sensibility of disappointment, loss, and injury mixed with alarmed responsibility. The feeling I took away was that here was a woman who had seen too much and been asked to do too much. Yet even now she seemed to be steeling herself for things to get worse, creating an aura of vulnerability that I had not ever before seen in Idi. She told me that over the last two years she had gone through terrifying encounters that had left her feeling drained and pushed against the wall. Up until this point, whatever emotions of frustration and failure she had felt had been transient. They were quickly sublimated into amused irony and soft, self-effacing criticism. But Idi now spoke as if her former confidence had dispersed, and along with it her hopes about her work and the world in general. She seemed bereft of her can-do optimism. In its place were grim emotions of loss, fear, and demoralization. These feelings mirrored grim on-the-ground conditions. In Sierra Leone, civil conflict, which had been going on since the early 1990s, seemed interminable. The military forces of the government competed with different rebel groups as to who could do greater damage to villages and towns. People were mutilated or killed, families broken apart, agricultural and market systems destroyed. Liberia was in even worse condition: the society, not just the state, was broken. In eastern Congo, the aftermath of the Rwandan genocide in 1994 sent large numbers of diverse groups into the rainforest. There were distinct militias, uprooted civilians, and Rwandan, Congolese, and other militaries. Their presence further destabilized this already highly decentralized region, so political control shifted frequently. Towns were occupied by one group of troops one month and then by another armed force the next. Violence was everywhere.

My concern only intensified when Idi observed, "I think I now have discovered how so many of my co-workers and predecessors became numbed. How people burn out and get out. It's pretty awful, really. Terrible, in fact. I was held at gunpoint not once but three times. I was repeatedly threatened. That's happened before. But not like this time. This time I thought I was going to be killed. I witnessed atrocities before. But not so many. Or with such a feeling of inadequacy. Sometimes it felt like nothing could be done. One side is as incapable of stopping as the other. And indeed there are always more than two sides. Everyone on the ground is complicit: the politicos, the militaries, the police, even the refugees. One minute you see a cute little kid, the next minute he holds an automatic rifle to your head and you feel he could care less whether you live or die. Even the UN people and the NGOs seem near helpless. So many are demoralized. The killings, the mutilation, the cycles of revenge, cease-fire after cease-fire, all the broken promises, wasted money, failed programs . . . the whole thing is rotting away. It is hyperdangerous, hypercorrupt, hyperthreatening."

Idi recounted fragments of her memories of the violence and destruction. In one town in the Congo, she had established a program for displaced women and children. When a new military force entered the town, all the women and children were forced to leave at gunpoint. Several days later a few women returned and reported being beaten and raped. In another market town, all the money Idi had brought in to pay for supplies and food was taken from her at gunpoint.

On yet another occasion, she barely avoided being beaten by Congolese government troops who were enraged over their losses in a recent battle and blamed her NGO for providing support for the militia they were fighting. Although she avoided being hurt, she had to resort to outright bribes to survive, leaving her with a profound sense of dismay.

"Never before have I had so much trouble controlling my reactions. I don't know if I know how to go on. My inside is numb and cold. I know I'm angry, very angry. But it's not like before. No hot rage. It's a cold, soul-freezing thing. Dead. I feel like part of me is dead. I feel my will is draining away. A failure, a fucking failure."

Here Idi was referring to the forced discontinuation of several of the programs she had started. She felt she was unable to provide support or protection for displaced families in great need. The core work of her NGO had stopped, as had that of the other NGOs. It was just too dangerous. The failure of her mission made her feel she had failed, so complete was her identification with her work.

Idi pursed her lips and stared at me. Her eyes grew moist. I felt as if she were staring straight through me. She seemed exhausted and lost. I sensed she might break down. I hurriedly (too hurriedly) suggested she take time off. Get away, I told her. Rethink this disaster and your role. Maybe do something else for a while as you sort out your options.

Idi just continued to look at me, unblinking. Then she bit her lip and wrinkled her nose into an expression of distaste. "No! I'm not going to run away. There are people, lots of people dependent on me. My NGO has a lot at stake. I can't walk away from that responsibility. I guess I'm talking to you about this stuff to find out what you can do when you feel numb and defeated but know you must go on. I don't know what will happen. Maybe this is the beginning of the end. But I need you to listen. There are lots of us who feel this way. I've read about post-tramatic stress disorder (PTSD) and we have all sorts of mental health people coming through. Some of the ones specializing in PTSD sound like used-car salesmen giving a pitch for a car that's got problems. I'm not convinced. I don't feel like I have an illness. This is, well, despair, I guess. I spent years learning what needs to be done to help people in desperate situations and how to do it. And here the situation is so bad, I feel desperate. We all do. Nothing seems to work. But that's too black and white. It's not exactly right. A few things look promising. Then conditions change, and . . . they don't look so promising anymore. Right now nothing does. But I sense things could change."

Idi was referring to a particular relief program she had been asked by her home office to discontinue because of the severity of the violence. She had disregarded the order and kept going. For a while the program had seemed to be stabilizing; then a new militia took over whose leaders simply shut her operation down. There was such a back-and-forth in the conflict, however, that there was a possibility one of the militias she had worked reasonably well with could soon regain control of this area, and her program would be up and running again.

"It is just damn exhausting. You can only be frightened for so long before you begin to feel, fuck it, let's admit we don't know what to do. Nor does anyone else, it appears to me. So it's time not to wallow in misery, but to pull back, regroup, rethink, but *not* get out. We need help from people like you [here Idi meant my psychiatric role] to deal with the numbing, the demoralization. But I'm going back. Actually, it's astonishing: a fair number of colleagues have gone through this thing and gone back. But first I need to work out what I can do better. How to assist others. That's what it's about at heart. My life gains its meaning from this work. The people need me and I need them, I guess. Now I must do what job I can. To do that I need to find a way out of this . . . a road out of this desolation."

We talked for long time, or Idi did. I knew my job was to listen, to give her space to say all the things she needed to get out. The theme of desolation—in the sense of wretched isolation, dejection, anguish, and despair—wove its way through her words. She asked me if she was depressed in a clinical sense. I said no, I didn't think so. She asked me if I would still respect her if she couldn't go on with her career. "Come on," I remember saying, "I respect you more than just about anyone. It won't change if you can't go back to that horrendous place. In fact, I don't want you to go back. I'm afraid something could happen. You could be seriously injured or killed. Please, you've done enough. Either wait until it is safer or leave for good now!"

Idi asked me what I thought was wrong with her. I told her I wasn't going to give her a psychiatric diagnosis. "If you really want to know, I think you are demoralized," I told her. "Not in the sense of depression, but in that of a moral crisis. You feel the burden of responsibility for your programs and yet you don't see clearly how you can carry out that responsibility. You don't see a way forward for yourself and your programs, yet your work matters more than anything else to you. And you have done more than could be asked of anyone, but it isn't enough, is it? So what are you doing? Paying back your grandfather's moral debts? Liberating your soul by washing the feet of the most despised? Getting ready for sainthood?" I tried to shock her into rethinking what she was doing. We went over and over the same ground. Then Idi got up from the old Harvard chair next to my desk and reached across to me, kissing her fingers and placing them on my forehead. "You don't know any more than I do, do you? But I can see the love in your eyes and hear the great concern for me in your voice. That's what I came for," she said, and this time a faint smile spread slowly across her freckled cheeks. "I know who I am here. Maybe I am working out family guilt and liberating my soul. So what? I take your point: it is a moral crisis. How to live a moral life? I once thought I knew. I don't now. I need to find my way again. Don't worry about me." These last words I didn't write down. I didn't need to. I can still feel them inside me.

I walked out of William James Hall together with Idi, crossed Harvard Yard, and waited as she got into a taxi at the queue in the square. Then she gave me a big, big smile, and the taxi pulled away from the curb and turned west toward Brattle Street. My feelings were tumbling. I felt reassured and empty at the same time. Maybe desolation is contagious, I mused. Or maybe I just saw my moral exemplar disappear, and I need to rethink who I am. What does it mean to live a moral life? After all, what really matters? Out of that last encounter with Idi and those unanswered questions came the impetus for this book.

And so, after a brief rest period with friends in western Massachusetts, Idi Bosquet-Remarque—shaken but reanimated—went back into the conflagration. I followed her reimmersion through mutual friends. At first, she veered between losing purpose and giving in and starting over anew with yet another action project. Finally, she steadied herself and rebuilt one of the programs she had initiated earlier, which had been overrun and temporarily abandoned. Along with her renewed sense of confidence and purpose, Idi's passion and sense of injustice returned. She wrote me a note about her anger toward media figures who helicoptered in and out of danger zones for hour-long photo opportunities without experiencing what she took to be the defining reality: the effort to exist day by perilous day in the midst of chaos. She also described her renewed admiration for those who could not helicopter away—the displaced and the local populations, including local experts. Despite the extreme hardships and uncertainty, they had to find ways to keep going and recover. She passed a message to me through a mutual friend that she had had the dubious pleasure of falsifying her college thesis's theory that aid workers didn't have to experience the conditions local people did and hence lived a kind of morally false life that was unsustainable. It was bloody difficult to be a foreign expert, and you were not protected emotionally, physically, or morally from the great dangers around you. As in so much else of living, she explained, there was no single pattern. People experienced life and worked their way through events differently. Trauma was real and consequential, but no one could say how it was some people remained strong while others crumbled, how some professionals stayed to face the struggle while others escaped, defeated. She had been wrong, she wanted me to know, to downplay in her thesis the importance of burnout; but she was also wrong, she now held, not to have recognized multiple outcomes. She insisted that professionals, like laypersons, are not necessarily best viewed as passive sufferers. Both are active agents who rework suffering, like so much else in life, into their own lives, private and professional. What mattered most was commitment. If you had it, you could stick it out; when you lost it, it was time to get out. I never had an opportunity to ask Idi to expand or clarify this point. So, like much in my life, it is a fragment buried deep in me that periodically irritates and needs to be massaged and thought through. Amidst great dangers and huge uncertainties, Idi seemed to be telling me, she had found what mattered most, and it was commitment to be there, for and with others who were in greatest need. Whatever its source or its consequences for her life, that commitment counted most; it was what she was, and what she felt she had to do.

Idi Bosquet-Remarque completed another year in Africa, returned to France, and moved to Switzerland to take up a temporary post with a European NGO. She was driving a rented car on a mountain road in winter in the French Jura when her car skidded and she was killed. It was a shock to all who knew her.

Later, when I told Idi's relatives that I intended to tell her story in a book I was writing, her mother and sister requested that I not reveal the family's identity and that I also alter some of the details of her life to protect her and their anonymity. "That way," her mother confided in our final telephone conversation, "you will honor what she believed in. Not saints

or heroes, but ordinary nameless people doing what they feel
they must do, even in extraordinary situations. As a family,
we believe in this too." Her sister offered a long lament that
ended with this encomium: "She was so splendid . . . in her
work and her being. Everything she did carried with it beauty.
She was beautiful in action—a kind of moral beauty. And you
know others sensed that, and it changed them. We've received
some wonderful letters from her friends and colleagues in
Africa and Asia. One was written by one of her very best
friends, an African woman whom Idi visited from time to time
to refresh her spirit and just have fun. I'm holding that letter
in my hands just now. It reads, 'Will the programs she
struggled so hard to build and save last? Who knows? Maybe
not. Did they make a huge difference in what is happening
here? No, of course not. How can a single person hold back a
flood? But did those programs make a difference for some
persons: yes, indeed, they did, they do. Will we miss her?
Very much. Will she be remembered and will that memory
matter: Yes! Among my husband's people there is the idea that
the ancestral spirits can include outsiders, like foreigners, who
can become a powerful source of energy and efficacy in the
lives of present and future generations. I feel Idi is one of them
and that his relatives must propitiate her spirit via rituals. I
have requested that and paid for the rites. So soon she shall be
here again among us, helpful as usual, beautiful as usual, lively
we hope as ever, doing good in the world.'"

Idi was remarkable because she was so serious in her commitment to assist people in danger. Idi regarded her own desperation as an accurate reflection of what most people on the
ground were experiencing: the personal trauma of a public

crisis. She worked in countries where the state had failed. There was no organization of services. Public order unraveled. The processes that define a functioning economy—buying, selling, traveling, farming, fishing—stopped. Going outside to collect firewood or drinkable water was a life-threatening task. The complete absence of social control gave rise to impunity for those who resolved feuds and rivalries with violence. In this setting there simply was no official presence—even a corrupt one—to negotiate with. Nothing that had broken got fixed. Terror was everywhere. The UN system and NGOs, worried about the safety of their staff, pulled out field workers and abandoned programs. Chaos was everywhere, thick on the ground.

Another field worker for a humanitarian assistance initiative described living and working in such countries in the starkest terms: "The saliva dries up in your mouth. Your heart is racing all the time. You imagine gangs of thugs and mercenaries coming after you. Your local staff melts away. Who could blame them. But it leaves you terribly exposed. Your headquarters wants you out of there, now. But really it's too late to get away, and even if you could, you know that your presence—thin and insubstantial as it is—may be the only thing separating the people you are there to protect from massacre. Try to run away from that one and think of what happens to any sense of decency and professionalism that guides your identity. It is the most godawful feeling. There is nothing, it seems, that you can do, but to leave is to maybe make things much, much worse."

He went on to say that when the killing started in a refugee camp in Sierra Leone where he was stationed, even this sentiment gave way to sheer terror and an almost reflexlike response to save himself first. I asked him if he had stayed after that. He looked hard into my eyes, then tears formed in his and he said no.

WHERE IS THE OUTRAGE, the demand for justice? Where is the impulse to assist others? Where is the commitment to doing good in the world? Idi's story, sad as its ending is, is about a life devoted to another image of what the world is like or could be like. As a college and medical school teacher, I have met more than a few students who started out with Idi's orientation. Over time most drop out as career and family concerns lead in entirely other directions. Yet some—a surprising number, in fact—stay the course and build lives like Idi's. They are vulnerable to the same moral experiences that so profoundly shook Idi. They rarely surface as moral exemplars (though a few, such as Paul Farmer and Jim Kim, do) because the media prefer a different kind of survivor and hero, a glamorous figure who dramatically triumphs against the odds in a clear-cut success story that brings lasting results.

And yet generation after generation have made this moral commitment, from the YMCA movement at the close of the nineteenth century through the Peace Corps volunteers starting in the 1960s and those today who work for international NGOs concerned with humanitarian assistance, medical aid, and human rights. These brave individuals take significant risks and commit themselves to causes that make their lives more difficult and volatile than they would be otherwise. Many experts in postcolonial studies believe that individuals such as Idi and humanitarian assistance in general actually deepen the very problems they seek to address. The humanitarian aid workers, either out of naivete or active collusion, it is claimed, camouflage the harsh consequences of the global political economy by suggesting that traditional values and foreign idealism will win out in the end. The focus is turned away from the political and economic processes that create such serious social problems as extreme poverty, systematic corruption, and political violence, sidetracking questions of land reform, improving access to education, providing effective health care and public health services, and replacing the cronyism and corruption of patrimonial politics with representative government and a free and critical press. Concern with the plight of particular individuals and families distracts from the proper focus on societal problems of inequality and destitution. What is more, these critics of humanitarian assistance argue, the values imported by the agents of humanitarian aid may subvert the agency of local communities and replace local moral experience with global commitments—such as the politically correct overemphasis on individual freedoms and the overvaluing of a culture of consumption—as a way of fostering not just Western power but Western moral superiority. The foreign institutions set an agenda that works for their purpose but may not work for individual countries. Indeed, the expatriate agenda may deepen social problems and make their alleviation more difficult. And expatriates may be as corrupt and corrupting as local power brokers.

Idi was not unaware of the bite of these criticisms. She herself referred to them and believed they were partially justified. But only partially. It was the quality of the human commitment to others in deep distress with full awareness of the moral complexities of that action that stood for her as the defining act of solidarity and practical assistance. It is a matter of what you see (or choose to see), she said, what you feel (or do not feel), what you end up doing (or find yourself not doing), how you practice living and what demands you make on where the world has (and can) take you. It is a matter, she went on, of what you can say back to the world and do in response to the world. It was her unselfish, admittedly difficult-to-defend, but perhaps still not entirely impractical conviction, tempered by wariness about unintended outcomes, that the world can be, must be changed. Her life demonstrated that this is what really mattered to Idi. And Idi herself mattered greatly to the few people who knew her well, including me, because, in the words of her sister, of the moral beauty of the life she envisaged and struggled to sustain.

4

Yan Zhongshu

"To survive in China you must reveal nothing to others. Or it could be used against you. Use only indirection and . . . ambiguous language. Sometimes you even should block your own thoughts, because you know at those terrible times you can't trust yourself. You might betray yourself and others. That's why I've come to think the deepest part of the self is best left unclear. Like mist and clouds in a Chinese landscape painting, hide the private part behind your social persona. Let your public self be like rice in a dinner: bland and inconspicuous, taking on the flavors of its surroundings while giving off no flavor of its own. Too strong a personal flavor and you may entice others to jealousy or hatred. Some will want to take advantage of what they know to get ahead and hurt you.

"You also need help from others so that no one can blame you. Strong connections can protect you and may offer a means of escape when you are trapped by circumstances. . . .

But a wife, a child, a close friend can also betray you. In your heart how can you be sure you won't betray them too?"

The speaker was Dr. Yan Zhongshu, a slight, white-haired retired physician seventy-six years of age who lives in Washington, D.C., with his unmarried daughter, a researcher in a small biotechnology firm. His two sons and their families still live in Beijing, the city where they and Dr. Yan himself were born and lived most of their lives. Dr. Yan has been in the United States for seven years but still does not feel entirely safe. He remains fearful that his family is vulnerable to persecution from the Chinese government should he say or do something that is perceived as against the Chinese Communist Party. Hence he insists that I use anonymity when telling his story: "I don't want my family's safety to be damaged."

I have known Dr. Yan for about a decade, beginning before he left China for the United States. We met at a medical conference, and we have had many talks, including formal interviews, most of which centered on the development of the medical profession in China. Some took place in my office at Harvard; a few were in his own home. In the course of these talks I learned a great deal about his life. Yan Zhongshu's story is salient to this book because it illustrates how history and politics and economics shape our moral lives, and because it also discloses that individuals in the worst of times can resist doing frightful things to others, even if the scope of that resistance is limited.

Dr. Yan continued: "I don't believe what anyone tells me unless they relate it to the actual conditions they have lived through. I know. I have had ideals. I have sworn not to follow bad models which I have seen all around me since childhood.

Yet in a bad time, I too was complicit. I did what I had to in order to survive.

"I imagine the situation has always been present to some extent in traditional Chinese society. Under Communism it has reached its most intense and awful stage. This is the constant pressure everyone in China must feel. . . . No one there can foretell what will happen next week, next month, or next year. For all we know policies could be entirely reversed. There could be another Cultural Revolution. You are shaking your head but you don't know. Of course it is unlikely, but no one can assure you—not with all the twists and turns we have taken under Communism—that it can't happen again. And in a different sense it has happened right now. Our age of market socialism is a cultural revolution of a different sort. What people believe in is reversed.

"You can attempt to read or control the future. But you can't. Only the Party and your work unit [each large workplace— factories, hospitals, universities—was organized as a work unit, where work and daily life activities were controlled by the all-powerful secretary of the local branch of the Communist Party] and people with great power can do that. And when times change, that is when you get hurt.

"In the years I have lived in America I have gone back to China three times. The reality of life, even with all the economic change, is the same. It may be a capitalistic market economy, but they can still go after you. When they do, only secrecy, and protection by others in your network, and fortune will determine what happens."

Dr. Yan was born in Beijing in 1929 into a small but rising merchant family, the youngest of five children including three sons. His grandfather and father built up an import-export business with branches in Shanghai, Tianjin, Guangzhou, and Hong Kong. From the late 1920s until 1937, while China was under the rule of the Nationalists (the Kuomintang, or KMT), the business thrived. Yan Zhongshu's grandfather first became a financial contributor to the KMT and later a KMT member. KMT-controlled gangs helped the family business to succeed. Dr. Yan observed sadly, "I don't know all that we did for the KMT, but I always suspected it was a lot and much of it illegal." After 1937, when the Japanese occupied Beijing and later still invaded other areas of China, including Shanghai, the Yans began to develop a behind-the-scenes relationship as collaborators. (From 1937 to 1945 the Japanese fought the KMT and their rivals, the Communists, in a brutal war during which the Japanese military occupied large parts of China and perhaps as many as twenty million Chinese were killed. The Japanese installed Chinese puppet authorities and forced businessmen, professionals, and other classes of Chinese to collaborate. In response, many from the Chinese elite class escaped to distant regions still under KMT or Communist control.) The Japanese authorities told Dr. Yan's grandfather and father that if they worked closely with the occupiers they would become even wealthier, and threatened to ruin their business if they did not. At the same time, KMT agents secretly visited the Yans and warned them that if they continued to collaborate openly with the Japanese they would be killed. Under mounting pressure from both sides, the entire family slipped away in the cold gloom of an early winter morning in 1940, and, led by KMT agents, made their way to Chongching, the damp, hilly, riverine city in the remote vastness of

Sichuan in China's southwest, where the KMT government had retreated in 1937 to continue the war with the Japanese invaders. In Chongching, the Yans were contacted by American advisors who eventually persuaded them to use their network of business agents to smuggle information out of and into Japanese-occupied territory. In 1945, after Japan's unconditional surrender following the atomic bombing of Hiroshima and Nagasaki, and with the surrender of all of Japan's military forces in China, the Yans returned to Beijing (then restored to KMT control) and resumed their trading activities. But as the conflict between the KMT and the Communists, led by Mao Zedong, turned into civil war and it became apparent that the Communists would win, the Yans negotiated with secret agents of the Chinese Communist Party (CCP) and began to send money, goods, and information to them. At the same time they kept their KMT ties active. "One of my uncles actually joined the [Communist] Party, but two others belonged to the KMT. . . . This was fairly common. You covered all the numbers on the gambling table with your bets. I abhorred this quality in my family. No ideals. No constancy. Blow with the wind. All that matters is to protect your wealth. In my mind I became a resister to this self-serving mentality. It seemed to me then to represent all that was wrong with the Chinese tradition."

In 1949, the Yans remained in Beijing after the Communist victory. At first they were warily optimistic about their prospects to survive and maintain their lifestyle under the new leadership, which reassured businessmen, professionals, and intellectuals that it would respect private property and other rights. But they soon heard that the CCP had begun the mass killing of landlords, and the Yans themselves began to feel the squeeze on their resources by CCP cadres. It very soon became clear that private property and businesses would be taken over by the state. In 1950, under the subterfuge of visiting their Guangzhou subsidiary to handle a business problem, the entire family escaped to Hong Kong. Yan Zhongshu was in medical school in Beijing at the time and decided, against the strongest family protest ("they tried to bribe me into joining them and into feeling guilty that I was unfilial"), to complete his schooling and remain in China afterward. "I rejected my family. I wanted to contribute to the motherland and work with all my might for values that were different than the commercial ones my family worshiped—values that led my family to collaborate with whatever power was in control no matter what they thought of it."

Dr. Yan told me that he believed Communist rule would be good for China because the new government would prioritize responding to the huge economic disparities, extreme poverty, and political chaos that had created so much suffering for the Chinese. "At first I felt good that I had made the right choice," Dr. Yan observed. "My classmates and I were truly enthusiastic about public policies that prioritized public health and social development. The government put an end to prostitution and with it the epidemic of STDs. They managed the drug abuse problem well too. Sale of female children was ended, as was female infanticide. The great migration of destitute peasants to the cities could be stopped because social order was reestablished. We created one standard of health care for everyone, at least in the cities. There was this great drop in infant mortality because of mass vaccination and sanitation.

The worst social health problems—TB, malaria, encephalitis, schistosomiasis—were coming under control. So were homelessness and extreme poverty. If you were a medical student with a progressive viewpoint—even one whose class interests seemed threatened—you had to be impressed. You know: the century had been China's shame. We were backward and ignorant; even India looked better. We were the sick man of Asia, and all of a sudden we were becoming something new and stable and promising. We could stand up and face the world and ourselves with pride."

But by the mid-1950s Dr. Yan, like most of his classmates and many other professionals, had second thoughts. They became disenchanted with land reform and urban renewal because of the brutality of the Communists' policy enforcement, which involved mass killings, forced expropriations, increasingly radical collectivization, and the imprisonment of critics and even those supporters who were suspected of not being enthusiastic enough. The propaganda of class warfare had hardened into repetitive abuse of people outside of the "red" sectors who now constituted a stigmatized "black" margin of class enemies: erstwhile businesspeople, homeowners, landowners, liberal intellectuals, and members of other political parties. Restrictions on living conditions tightened with rationing and reallocation of living space. Most irksome was the widening gap between the CCP's ultraegalitarian rhetoric and the actual practices that preferentially benefited the new cadre class, who had their own schools and higher-quality stores as well as special access to better housing. It seemed to Dr. Yan and his circle of friends that the revolution had merely changed membership in the elite class without doing away with it. Certainly, the takeover had not constructed an egalitarian society, which the increasingly strident political rhetoric claimed to be the aim of Communism.

In response to worsening political oppression, Dr. Yan surreptitiously made his way to Guangzhou, from where, assisted by his family's old network of business connections, he was smuggled into Hong Kong. But once inside this bastion of the British empire's capitalist policies, Dr. Yan did not at all feel liberated. Rather, he became ever more unhappy as he experienced a colonized society that displayed many of the social and economic ills that he associated with China under the KMT.

"I felt the Chinese in Hong Kong were exploited. My family, who had collaborated with the KMT and the Americans and the CCP, and had tried to do the same with the Japanese, were doing what they were good at, getting along with occupiers. There was no idealism at all, just the rush for money. I felt very uncomfortable, like I didn't belong. I thought I felt better in China, as difficult as the situation there had become, because at least in China there was a shared sense of undergoing hardship for some greater purpose, to build the nation. Socialism was oppressive to be sure, but it was *for* public health, social reform, accessible clinical care—all the right things. Capitalism stood for none of this, but rather seemed to thrive on greed, selfishness, and all the other bourgeois evils I had been taught in medical school to condemn. Here they all were. And my family was in the midst of it, pushing and shoving for money. I know it sounds foolish now, but at that time I regarded them as the essence of all that was old and ruinous in Chinese culture."

So, once again against the strenuous objections of his family members ("they almost locked me up"), Yan Zhongshu returned to China. The year was 1957. The terrible irony is that this young, idealistic physician from a wealthy family returned to China at the very moment radical Maoism was intensifying collectivization and the use of terror, like that deployed by Stalin in the Soviet Union two decades earlier, to control those perceived as unenthusiastic foot draggers, critics, dissenters, and outright enemies of the state. In the Anti-Rightist Campaign of 1957, which saw tens of thousands of intellectuals, professionals, and people whose class background made them suspect sent to labor camps or prisons, Maoist investigators interrogated Dr. Yan because of his bourgeois background and "overseas problem," meaning that he had family in Hong Kong. He came through the investigation without being branded outright a rightist, which would have meant years of stigma that would have put his life on hold, constant criticism, and perhaps time in a reeducation-through-labor camp (a euphemism for China's gulag of remote concentration camps for political prisoners), but he was under a pall of suspicion, viewed as potentially unreliable because of his family's involvement with the KMT and move to Hong Kong. "Had I received the label of a counterrevolutionary, as did several of my classmates, it would have meant prison, maybe a labor camp, or even a bullet in the back of the neck. Being a rightist outright would also have been pretty bad. Being a suspected sympathizer but not wearing a political cap, I was suspect and a target for criticism. I couldn't join the Party or advance my career professionally, of course. But after going through criticism and reeducation meetings—lots of them—I was allowed to continue as a doctor, though demoted from research to ordinary practice. That was okay with me. I enjoying seeing patients and was good at it. The really hard part was when my girlfriend was forced by her cadre family [cadres are local political officials] to renounce me. That made me feel bitter at the time, but eventually I came to accept this condition too as tolerable. I was after all only a little rightist, and there were mitigating circumstances. In fact, the Party branch secretary in the work unit did a lot to protect me. I was a good clinician and a hard worker. The hospital needed me. I survived. Probably if I had been in my girlfriend's situation, I would have done the same thing. I was raised to compromise and collaborate to get by, and under Communism I learned out of necessity how to do what I had resisted in my own family.

"I think that's what Communism had done to the Chinese people. Better than in ancient China under Confucian ideology, Communism forced people to learn how to accommodate those in power. Chinese like me—especially those who lived through the political campaigns—learned how to get by. You do what you must do . . . even if you can't stand what you did. But we also learned to be skeptical, skeptical of any ideology, especially Communism but including Confucianism. It is really much more than skepticism. We feel alienated from any standard of values. Only those that count at the moment to help you get through mean something. Take *guanxi* [connections traditionally based on either moral or pragmatic relations]. It's become entirely functional, pragmatic. The same with filial respect [filial reverence for parents and ancestors was the core of Confucian values]. The sentiment is if they aren't useful now, toss them away. It's a corruption of what they once meant. This is the saddest and most unfortunate legacy of Maoism. What these people have done to our tradition and to us. "

Stigmatized and restricted in opportunity to build the life and career he wanted, yet still "getting by," Yan Zhongshu unexpectedly received another chance to leave China. The year was 1965, the year before the onset of the most violent and chaotic political campaign that radical Maoists unleashed, this time against the leadership and the state itself, which Mao had come to view as resisting his policy of continuous revolution and challenging his power. "My family somehow managed to bribe a group of high-level cadres in Guangzhou through their old business networks. How they accomplished this, I still don't know, but they had the connections to do it. I might have gotten out. Who knows? I was suspicious of a setup. The police did that sometimes. Later I discovered it was the real thing, but by then the Cultural Revolution [1966–1976, a catastrophic, nationwide, political campaign that attacked individuals in the government, Party members, cadres in work units and particularly intellectuals who were labeled enemies of the people and often exiled to impoverished rural areas for political reeducation] had created near total chaos and it wasn't possible to even dream any longer of getting away."

In spite of the menacing atmosphere of the opening months of the Cultural Revolution, when Red Guards—radicalized youth—held public criticism sessions where political targets were beaten or even killed, Yan Zhongshu still believed he could contribute to build public health and health services for China and thereby "serve the people." Dr. Yan told me that to give himself courage he added up all the positive aspects of his situation, which even then seemed to him a pathetic way of trying to convince himself of his safety. At the top of the list was his professional competence as an infectious-disease expert. Surely, he told himself, medical experts such as he were needed, and his career would protect him from ostracism and injury. His experience in the early 1960s contributed to his denial and blindness to what was to come.

"The campaigns against rightists had relaxed. I was able to marry [a fellow physician in the same work unit with the same political problem of coming from a wealthy background and having family overseas]. We had two sons and she was pregnant again with our daughter. I was getting ahead in the hospital. It seemed to me things were getting better. What a miscalculation! I simply couldn't face up to how bad things were and how dangerous they were going to become."

In 1966 the Cultural Revolution quickly picked up speed, like a whirlwind, and Dr. Yan, his wife, and their children were sucked into the devastation. "It was truly horrible. Worse than I can convey. My wife was the target of a big character poster." These large posters placed in public spaces by radicalized members of the work unit attacked other members and targeted them for violent "struggle sessions," big public events that often involved everyone in the work unit. Either Red Guards from outside the unit or those radicalized work unit members who became Red Guards orchestrated these sessions, which were scripted to include denunciations by "the masses" of the politically targeted members, then forced self-criticism, followed by humiliation and beating of these "enemies of the people." Colleagues and family members were often forced to join in the criticism.

"She was beaten so badly one of her eyes was seriously injured. The retina had a tear and no one could help her. They [the work unit's Red Guards] kept her in the basement of the hospital in a kind of prison for several months. When she was released she had lost much of the vision in that eye and had developed a psychiatric condition. She was fearful all the time; even a noise frightened her so severely she didn't want to leave our apartment. Then they sent her to a rural area in the northeast. It took me a month to discover where she was. Meanwhile I had three small kids. I asked my in-laws to take care of my youngest, our daughter. Then with my two sons I went to a remote county in Gansu [in China's far west]. It was just as well, because life in China became completely chaotic. You couldn't get what you needed to care for a family: food meant standing in long lines for hardly any choices. There was no work. My clinical work stopped. So did my teaching and a research project I had started. A revolutionary committee of workers, students, and the military ran our hospital. Doctors like me who had political problems spent all their time in criticism sessions. No time to see patients. They beat us up and turned nurses on doctors, doctors against cadres, husbands against wives. It was truly a mass psychosis. Gansu was rough but in a different way."

Dr. Yan lived in a small town in Gansu from 1966 to 1972. From 1972 to 1976 he lived and worked in a large city in Gansu at a general hospital. "I lived with my sons for six years in a very difficult place. A rundown county town with limited electricity, insufficient and uneatable food in collective canteens.

We were always hungry. But what was really bad was that we had to drink brackish water. My hair fell out. I developed a skin disease. My older son didn't grow normally but seemed stunted. He was sick all the time. I was frightened he would die. Then when things got a little better in our living arrangements, I realized there was no schooling. So he learned about fixing tractors. That's about all. He lost his education, as did my second son, who even today seems cognitively slow. Somehow my daughter managed to come through all right in spite of the fact my in-laws, who took care of her, had by then become street cleaners.

"I couldn't stand my situation. The poverty was crippling. We had almost no equipment or drugs. Here I was a high-tech expert and I watched patients die from routine infections because we couldn't get antibiotics. I was an intellectual and there was nothing to read. No one to talk to about ideas. I felt like my mind was drying up. Periodically some cadres came through to attack those of us who were under a political cloud. There was yelling and screaming. You were made to feel terrible . . . frightened, agitated, lost. You couldn't say where things were going. Some days the complete absence of stimulation made you feel a quick death would be preferable. But slowly I gained the confidence of local leaders who really appreciated my dedication to practice good medicine in such bad conditions. They sent us more to eat. We got a place to live that was not so terrible. They protected me from visiting bands of Red Guards. What they couldn't do was lessen my fear or desperation. I thought about suicide. But what good would that be for my children—and wife? We were survivors, my family; somehow I felt I'd get through, but it was terrible. So bad that when I think about the dirt, the awful and meager food, the dirty, sour water, I feel that old despair again like a numb, empty feeling, a terrible feeling I don't ever want to relive again. Ah, what a time!

"Meanwhile my wife's mental condition continued to deteriorate. I couldn't get permission for her to join us in Gansu or for me or her parents to visit her in the northeast. I felt so frustrated. I think it was that that made my hair begin to fall out and then turn white. In the fourth year of our separation, I received word that she had committed suicide. I never saw the body or got the details. Was it true? Was she murdered? No one could find out. It was all so very inhuman. I became very bitter. I could be surly with my sons and with my patients. I was filled with anger and grief. I was hopeless. Well, not exactly. If I had been hopeless, I would have agreed to remarry. 'A true peasant wife,' the leaders of the county hospital told me. I resisted and fortunately was able to avoid that or I would still be in Gansu.

"They needed my skills, and I knew that. But there was a danger to being effective. They wanted to keep me. [The local CCP leaders had complete control over Dr. Yan and his children.] Meanwhile, others were returning to their homes in Beijing, and I was still living in that hell. But I had made up my mind. I would get away one day by whatever means; I'd get out. That was the only hope I had, and it kept me alive."

Soon after the Cultural Revolution officially came to its end in 1976, Dr. Yan together with his sons returned to Beijing. He had been able to bribe several of the local cadres responsible for personnel to authorize his application for a transfer. At the same time his hospital's leaders in Beijing were attempting to resurrect their infectious-disease program. They invited him to return, and the local authorities complied. Beijing it-self was in difficult straits: warring political factions had brought work units to a standstill, schools and universities had stopped operating, and Dr. Yan's hospital was in disre-pair. In 1978, with Deng Xiaoping's declaration of a new era of economic reform, Yan Zhongshu received news that he was officially rehabilitated. As a direct result, the director of the hospital promoted him to a senior post. This time his career—both as a clinician and a clinical teacher—flourished. Together with younger colleagues who were quick to master the new laboratory techniques, he undertook clinical research studies that have been published in China's leading medical journals and several times in European and American research reports.

"I tried to make up for all those wasted years. We all did. But it was too late for my sons to catch up educationally. At first I considered this to be one more tragedy, but actually, since advancement was blocked for higher education, they were encouraged by the new economic conditions to be among those who tried new things. They were ready as jobs opened in the private sector to take advantage of what for others was a risky adventure." In the early years of the economic reform, 1978 to the mid-1980s, it was young people on the margins of society, such as Dr. Yan's sons—who did not work in the then more desirable, guaranteed jobs of the public sector and who did not have the education to advance through the univer-sity system—who entered into the newly opened and quite uncertain opportunities of the private sector. Called "jump-ing into the sea," starting up or joining private companies was risky, but out of this generation of entrepreneurs emerged the real vanguard of China's extraordinary economic success in the past two decades. "They [his sons] started off working in restaurants. Then they joined a shipping company. Eventually they went back to their roots and found work in a new import-export firm. Now they have support from their cousins in Hong Kong, and the business is successful, and they have moved up to managerial positions. They plan to start up a branch of the old family business, which already is operating in different parts of China, sometimes with the children or grandchildren of those who were the original business agents. They are doing well, and my grandchildren will receive the education denied to them.

"My daughter followed a completely different path. She did well in school. By the time she was in senior middle school the question of class background no longer mattered so much for admission to university. Staying in Beijing with her grandparents, her education wasn't disrupted to the extent of those sent to rural areas, like my sons. She received a reasonable science background at the university, and she graduated at a time when American universities were seeking out Ph.D. students in the sciences and engineering from China. Getting a visa proved to be no big problem because by then lots of Chinese were going to America. She got her Ph.D. in biology from the University of California and then did several postdocs at East Coast universities. One of her mentors went on to join a small biotechnology firm, and so she went too. She is a very hard worker, like me, and she is well paid. She chose not to marry. I am still hopeful, but she says she isn't interested in marriage. I managed to come to America to live with her after I retired. My family in Hong Kong sent me money and asked me to retire in Hong Kong. I visited a few times, but eventually I thought it would be better for me to be with my daughter. She looks like my wife and I want to help her, and she wants me to share her life. We don't need to talk about the past, but it's with us all the time, like a shared scent."

Dr. Yan's eyes teared; he shook his head, coughed, and went on. His voice sounded soft and sad at first, but it quickly changed, becoming hard and insistent.

"It makes me dizzy and weak to think of the past and all that has happened. Today it seems like traditional ideas about the cycles of history are coming true. China is more or less back to where it was in the 1930s. My sons are doing what my grandfather and father did. And the Communist Party is still in command. But who could have imagined this during the Cultural Revolution? It is a strange kind of progress. My generation was blown apart. Lives ended. Careers were stopped. Families were destroyed. Look at what happened to my wife. Look at me. I got through it, somehow, but what a terrible waste of years. So much misfortune! Ah! But this new time is troubling in its own way. So many of the problems of the 1930s have returned: drug abuse, prostitution, homelessness, unemployment, corruption. Corruption, I think, is the worst problem. The whole country runs by corruption. . . . You want to buy something, pay someone off first. You want the police to do their job, you've got to pay them. Medicine was never so corrupt. Probably because we had so little money earlier, and if you had it then, what would you buy? Now you need money all the time. Patients must give bribes to see a specialist or to get surgery or the latest medicines.

"I told you how I hated the way my family collaborated with this faction or that one. But really I now wonder, is there any other way? We've all become like that. Communism ruined so much in China. Who can look at China now without feeling regret? So much pain and injury to produce a society that is crude, greedy, and empty of values. Everything is superficial and pragmatic. You scratch my back, then I scratch yours. If you don't help me, I drop you and move on to cultivate someone else. If he doesn't help, I drop him too. Everything for sale. No more big lies because no one even believes in Communism. But capitalism looks dirty and disappointing. It's not the capitalism of the States but something wilder, rougher. There was a bitter joke in Beijing before Tiananmen. What's the longest and most painful road to capitalism? Yes, you've got it . . . Communism. But nowadays the bitterness has disappeared and so has the idealism. Where is China headed? What's happening to the Chinese people? Nothing could be worse than Maoism, but the current direction is destructive too."

Dr. Yan continued with a bitter smile: "Let me tell you a story. When the Cultural Revolution broke out, I had a close friend in my clinical department. He and I graduated from the same medical school. He was the classmate I felt closest to. He had a very open personality. We had many good times together. He actually introduced me to my wife. I helped him advance in the hospital. He was very ambitious. We spent our free time together. Once when we were drinking together we swore an oath to be like blood brothers and protect each other and our families. He came from a different background. His parents were ordinary workers. They were poor. So Xu

Weiqing came from a red background. But he also had a political problem. His uncle had been forced by the authorities
to become a soldier in the KMT army. Eventually his uncle
became an officer and escaped to Taiwan, where he rose to a
high rank. I knew this and other things about my friend, and
he knew just about all there was to know about me. We had
sworn to keep these secrets, and I trusted him. Then during
the Cultural Revolution, there was a big struggle session in
the hospital. A lot of the senior doctors were attacked. But
after a few weeks the criticisms began to include more junior
staff. Then I became a target. I got criticized." Dr. Yan was
criticized both for the old political issues of his class background and his family in Hong Kong and because his science
orientation was said to reflect too urban and elitist an ideo-
logical orientation. "Weiqing was attacked for being my friend.
He was told [by the unit's Red Guards] to draw a clear line
between us. And after being roughed up and threatened with
being sent to some horrible place in the remote mountains,
he ended up . . . hmm, denouncing me. That was bad enough.
But he did more to hurt me. He revealed everything I had
told him, which got me into such serious trouble that only
the party secretary saved my life by moving me and the boys
to Gansu. Otherwise I was done for." Dr. Yan was close to the
leaders of the hospital, including the party secretary, because
they valued him as one of the best clinicians and also for his
high scientific standards.

"I just couldn't accept what Weiqing did. Lots of friends
were forced to turn on each other. Even married couples. You
had to make a show of it or you were attacked. But friends
usually said the least they had to. Two of my other friends

did just that. They joined the denunciations, but even though they could have worsened the case against me and gotten me into more serious trouble, they kept quiet about the more dangerous things they knew about me. Weiqing told everything. He even embellished the truth so that I looked really bad. It was Weiqing who yelled first that I could never be trusted but was an enemy of the people who should be beaten to death. He grabbed a stick and hit me with it. He really meant to injure me. I fell down bleeding. There were hundreds of people present. The Red Guards urged him on. But most of the work unit members were silent. I think Weiqing could have killed me if he had been allowed to continue to hit me. My head was bleeding. My arm was numb. Then two senior doctors who were still respected stepped forward at the urging of the party secretary. They took the stick away from him. They pushed me into a storage room. The party secretary locked the door. I was covered in blood. My glasses were broken. I could feel the blood trickle down the back of my neck where the skin was raw from the beating. Weiqing hit me so hard on the head I had a gash that required stitches. But I felt no pain. My heart was filled with sadness and grief. Later still anger flooded through me. I hated him for betraying me and nearly killing me—all to protect himself.

"Well, years later when I returned from Gansu, we were again in the same department. In fact, we shared an office. I couldn't look at him or speak to him. I detested him. I blamed Weiqing for everything that had befallen me, even what happened to my wife. Because he had accused her too. I felt a burning in my chest rising into my throat, just being around him. Under my breath I cursed him: 'You bastard, when I get the chance, I'll get back at you!' But never so that he or anyone else could hear. I'd learned my lesson. Never trust anyone!

"Well, in 1982, I think it was, Weiqing finally came up to me and tried to apologize. He couldn't justify what he had done, of course, but he tried to make it sound ordinary, as if everyone did what he did. You remember, it was just after the time of the literature of scars [a short period in which novels, short stories, and actual personal narratives of suffering during the Cultural Revolution were authorized by the Party]. All sorts of personal accounts appeared condemning the terrible things that had taken place in the Cultural Revolution. After a year or so the authorities stopped it, because the criticism was getting out of control. But still a lot of people were trying to come to terms with all that had happened. Several friends, for example, told me how sorry they were. How they tried to protect me but couldn't. I didn't believe them completely, but I could understand their situation. Weiqing was different. He had told everything and almost killed me, and what he said to justify his actions was simply untrue. I said nothing in return. He couldn't look at me when he spoke. He had no face [that is, he had no moral standing]. I turned away from him.

"About four years later, I had the chance I dreamed about to get revenge. The hospital had a connection with a rural commune in a very poor area of Henan [an impoverished interior province]. When they could, they provided us with fruits, and we sent them medicine. Under pressure from the government to help rural areas, the leaders of our hospital decided to reopen a clinic in that commune that members of our department had staffed during the Cultural Revolution.

They badly needed a full-time clinical director who would make a commitment of several years. It was a terrible position, a kind of exile. It would finish off the research career of whoever went there. It would also be a very difficult place to live. No one wanted to go. Everyone looked for an excuse. The party secretary, who had at last been rehabilitated and reinstated after a terrible ordeal like mine, came to see me. He too had been criticized and beaten by Weiqing. He said to me that now was the time to get back at him. 'We can kill him,' he snarled, 'by having him sent to that place. He has asthma and will never survive there. When we have the big meeting to choose a head of the clinic, you propose Weiqing. Everyone will support you. That's all you need to do. I'll take care of the rest, and we'll get the bastard for good.'

"Now, Weiqing was an excellent physician and researcher. His career was really flourishing. He had big ambitions but was somewhat thwarted by his past. People remembered his actions in the Cultural Revolution—against me, against the party secretary and others—no one trusted him. He had lots of enemies among the senior staff, otherwise he would already have been appointed department head. This was what I had waited for, the opportunity to finish him off.

"The meeting took place at night. The hospital's main auditorium was filled. There was a lot of excitement and anxiety. Everybody was scared of being sent to that remote clinic. The party secretary asked for nominations. He looked at me. I felt all my hatred focus on the words that would recommend Weiqing. I saw him squirm. He knew it was a setup. He knew I was going to get revenge. That the party secretary would make it happen. He couldn't look up. His eyes were fixed on the floor. You could see his body tremble. The party secretary coughed. He looked at me as if to say, 'Get on with it. What are you waiting for? Let's get him out of the way.' Finally, out of frustration, he called my name: 'Comrade Yan has something to say.'

"I looked at Weiqing. I felt my face flush, my heart pound. I started sweating. Meanwhile, I could slowly recall the terrible day when Weiqing betrayed me and almost killed me. 'Comrade Secretary,' I blurted, 'it is too much for any of us to stay in that remote commune for years. It would be like going back in time to the worst days of the Cultural Revolution. Comrade Deng Xiaoping says that a cat can be black or white. It doesn't matter so long as it catches mice. Let us not send anyone out there like I was sent to Gansu and you were sent to Xinjiang. No more vengeance. No more name-calling. No more destroying lives and careers. I recommend instead that we rotate the position every few months among the staff. I'm ready to go for a month. So should everyone else.'

"I really can't say how I said those words. I can't remember making a decision to say them. They just came out, like an explosion. But I wasn't unhappy with what I said. Surprised, but not unhappy. No sooner did I finish speaking than dozens of staff members—senior and junior—yelled their support. There was so much agreement that the party secretary could do nothing but agree too. There was an atmosphere of relief. At any rate, that became the policy. I became a small hero. And the opportunity to get back at Weiqing disappeared like that."

Yan Zhongshu put his head back, resting it on the large armchair in the study of the apartment in Washington, D.C., he shared with his daughter. His face seemed to me calmer. He closed his eyes. I thought he had fallen asleep. But just then he began to speak in a soft, slow manner. "Retrospectively it seems incredible, just like you say. But I think I've come to understand myself. I could never hurt anyone like Weiqing hurt me. It must be constitutional. Even during the worst days of the Cultural Revolution, I couldn't bring myself to attack others. I made believe a few times. But my colleagues knew I was only pretending. And many were that way too. The ruthless ones were those sad cases who completely lost themselves in the mass hysteria and were capable of doing the worst things. Some had great cruelty in their hearts, but most were acting out of fear. They felt threatened and fought to survive. That was a fairly sizeable group, but still a minority . . . most of us just went through the routines. Weiqing was so very ambitious that he forgot about others. What I think is that he became terrified of what might happen to him if he didn't protect himself, and to do that he needed to get rid of me. Actually, he told me as much after the big meeting at the hospital. He came to my apartment. There were tears in his eyes. He knocked his head on the ground to thank me. He called himself names: coward, bastard, things like that. He told me he had felt trapped and needed to protect himself. He would do anything he had to do to survive, no matter what. He sacrificed me to keep himself alive. Then when he had betrayed the secrets I told him, he lost himself in a terrible rage, he said. He hated me for putting him in that position and he hated himself for what he was doing. And he was afraid. Afraid I would turn on him and afraid that association with me would ruin his chances.

Weiqing told me that at that moment he truly wanted to kill me and would have if he wasn't stopped.

"We never spoke again about that time. We worked together for years. There was a superficial return to speaking terms. We joked together a few times and we even took a few meals together. But whenever I thought of my poor wife, or my sons and me drinking that sickening brackish water, I felt ice in my heart. I could not forgive him. I did not trust him. And so I would not be too friendly, despite all his efforts. That [instinct] proved right a few years later."

From April 1989 to early June of that year, during China's "democracy spring," demonstrators in the enormous public space of Tiananmen Square demanded greater political freedom for China and openly criticized the government and the Party. Over time the numbers grew from hundreds of students to thousands of Chinese of every class, background, and occupation. Entire work units marched under the banners of democracy and freedom: universities, factories, newspapers. Citizen groups in different areas leading into and out of this central public space—before the Forbidden City (for hundreds of years home of China's emperors), beside the mausoleum holding Mao's embalmed body, next to the Great Hall of the People, and only blocks from the gated community where China's current rulers reside—blocked major roads, preventing police and military units from entering. Smaller demonstrations took place in other Chinese cities. The political order was under assault. Leading government officials met with student leaders of the protest, but were unable to restore order or control the situation, which looked to be spinning toward breakdown of the Communist dictatorship as was happening in Russia and Eastern Europe. During this same period the press became more critical of the political system and books and films appeared (for example, *River Elegy*) that criticized not only Chinese Communism but the entire Chinese cultural tradition as being oppressive, corrupt and anti–human rights.

Finally, the retired senior leader—Deng Xiaoping—together with a powerful circle of colleagues, who were staunchly antireform and feared that the state would collapse if something were not done to break the democracy movement, rallied the military and struck back, killing hundreds and perhaps thousands of students, workers, and other ordinary citizens while clearing Tiananmen of its newly erected liberty statue and all other symbols of protest and change. Then there followed a brief but brutal period of repression as the Party sent authorities to identify, imprison, and in some cases execute leaders of the movement, a number of whom escaped Beijing for the countryside or other cities, or even made their way to Hong Kong and the West. There would be no peaceful revolution from below, no change of the political status quo in China.

Dr. Yan initially hesitated to participate in the demonstrations. He remembered back to the Hundred Flowers Campaign of the late 1950s when Mao invited criticism of the government and the Party, but when it became too widespread and serious, he instigated a campaign against the critics who had let their ideas be publicly known. Cynics had said that Mao's original intention had been to smoke out his critics and target them for repression. So Dr. Yan was wary as the democracy movement accelerated into a full-scale assault on Communist society. But near the end of May, as virtually the entire staff of his hospital took part in the demonstrations, he joined a doctors' march, one of whose leaders was his old friend the party secretary, who was now about to retire. Following the June 4 massacre, a period of repression and recrimination began. An investigation squad of police visited the hospital and interrogated activists, including the party secretary. Somebody had denounced the work unit's leaders as politically incorrect. Months later it emerged that Xu Weiqing was the informer. Only modest trouble resulted from the investigation, but it did delay the party secretary's retirement and may have cost him some of his benefits. Several years later the party secretary told Dr. Yan that he had learned from his connections in the police that Xu Weiqing had been an informer since the early days of the Cultural Revolution. He pointed out that had Dr. Yan acted at the right moment, Xu Weiqing would have been exiled and would not have been able to continue to cause trouble. Dr. Yan responded with rage and criticized himself so passionately for being naïve and stupid that the party secretary had to calm him down. "I will not be fooled again," Dr. Yan swore at the time. "But in fact I was," he sighed to me, and continued: "And that's how I began to understand more clearly what China is becoming."

Promoted to be deputy head of his clinical department in 1991, Dr. Yan was responsible for overseeing clinical services. The 1990s were a difficult time for China's hospitals, and Dr. Yan's hospital was no exception. Costs of electricity, basic supplies, medical equipment, and food increased rapidly, but the government forced hospitals to charge patients the same outpatient registration fee and inpatient per diem as they had earlier. At the same time, the Ministry of Health and its local urban equivalents reduced support for the salaries of hospital staff, the procurement of drugs, and the maintenance of older buildings and the construction of new ones. The hospital where Dr. Yan practiced was caught in a crunch. The huge migration of rural workers to the city increased emergency ward and outpatient visits. Hospital staff were underpaid and overworked.

   In addition, the market economy changed the balance of power in the patient-doctor relationship and, indeed, the entire medical profession. An authoritarian Confucian model that gave primacy to doctors was transformed into a consumer model that encouraged patients to request the latest and more costly diagnostic tests and treatments. The hospital's leaders pressed clinicians to pander to this desire for high technology, as they saw it as one of the only ways of meeting their financial obligations. Thus doctors were encouraged to engage in bad clinical practices such as ordering tests that were unnecessary, overpriced, and potentially dangerous. On the treatment side, doctors were told to prescribe more drugs and to favor the most expensive ones. Much the same took place with surgical interventions. Patients and families, exposed to the media's hyping of the marvels of biomedicine, were willing participants in what Dr. Yan regarded as systematic abuse of professional standards and a misuse of scarce resources.

   The changing climate within medicine encouraged not only inefficiency and wastefulness but also mass corruption. Senior doctors with established reputations had such a large following of patients that they would see new patients only if they received a suitable "gift," usually a bundle of cash in a paper bag or envelope placed at the doctor's side. Surgeons expected such gifts before and after operations. "Money became everything," Dr. Yan lamented. "For the administrators, including the new party secretary, it was the measure of success. For doctors and nurses, it was necessary to live in the new market economy. Before, there was little to buy, and you didn't need to pay for most things—rent, food, services were either part of what the work unit provided or were deducted from your salary. Now you need money to buy things, and you are expected to pay for everything yourself. Buying things is what China is now about. It is like a complete reversal of how things were in the era of collectivization. Corruption is completely out of control, like before 1949. The drivers of the ambulances demand bribes to bring a sick person to the hospital. The hospital porters expect a small tip to show families where to go to register or visit a ward. The policemen at the gate won't let cars enter let alone park without collecting a little 'gift.' None of this is appropriate. Even the medical students and medical school teachers get involved. Our best students, the smartest and most ambitious, who formerly would have gone into research and specialty practice, now prefer to work in the pharmaceutical industry. They sell drugs to the hospital's doctors and give kickbacks to those doctors who prescribe their drugs the most. The teachers expect money for after-hours tutorials, and they make it clear that if you want to pass exams, you better take these extra courses."

Dr. Yan found himself becoming increasingly discouraged. "I couldn't accept what was happening. People regarded me as a foolish idealist. I couldn't believe we had spent all those years emphasizing collective values and high standards only to sink into selfishness and corruption. It was completely demoralizing. And not just for me. My friends and colleagues also complained. We actually had believed the ideology: 'serve the masses,' 'build the nation,' 'strive selflessly to assist comrade workers and peasants.' Now that it has all changed, it makes the past seem false, a big lie.

"I used to be a consultant to a special ward at a hospital in the late '70s that was set aside for senior cadres. It had air-conditioning, the latest technology, high-class food, maid service, while the rest of the hospital's wards were crumbling. But even though we knew there was inequality, we still believed in the collectivist rhetoric, believed it made us superior to capitalism. With the change in the economy in the 1990s, we became what we had been taught to criticize. This was the true 'cultural revolution.' At first it seemed great. We had clothing that was much nicer, new places to eat, better living conditions, opportunities to travel, even abroad. But over time it has returned us to all the evils of the 1930s. Businessmen tell us that China in the twenty-first century is like America was at the end of the nineteenth century, the 'wild West.' You can buy everything, even people. Everything is for sale.

"Now that I live with my daughter here in America, I realize China's brand of capitalism is much cruder than America's. People are materialistic and pragmatic and that's it. Americans may take that for granted, but you have religion and spirituality. And there is a legal system and a moral code. In China the situation is worse, much worse. Traditional cultural practices are empty and dying. There is no religion. Qigong is a search for that, but it is very thin and superficial. What can you expect from the one-child family and all the materialism? There is so much selfishness. It is the time for people like Xu Weiqing. My time is over. But the time for scoundrels is now."

Clearly Dr. Yan's bitterness over the wasted years, the cultural hypocrisy, and continuing political oppression colored his view of breathtaking economic changes that have catapulted China from a poor country to the world's third largest economy and an engine of growth for the global political economy. This has vastly altered the lifeways of ordinary Chinese, especially the 250 million Chinese who live in the coastal cities and special economic zones, which have experienced such a huge economic transition. While there is still plenty of criticism of the failure of political reform, Chinese inside and outside China have increasingly become robustly nationalistic and are viewing the period of economic reform as an era of unprecedented prosperity that has altered not only material realities but the very meaning of what it is to be Chinese. The fact that China will be hosting the Olympic Games in 2008 is seen by many as symbolic of this new era of its international power and optimistic internal transformation. So while he is not alone in his criticisms, Dr. Yan is considerably more negative about the new China than most commentators, inside and outside China, for whom bitterness over the radical Maoist past is being replaced by the sense that China is entering an epoch of enormous possibility.

Dr. Yan's career began to wind down in the early 1990s when there was tremendous financial pressure on the hospital. The new party secretary and new director of the hospital held a meeting with the senior physicians and told them the hospital faced financial ruin unless it found new ways of generating money. Some of Dr. Yan's colleagues suggested that they copy other, more famous hospitals, which were opening up clinics intended for rich overseas Chinese and other foreigners. The approach would be to charge inflated amounts for the latest high-tech diagnostic and therapeutic procedures. Dr. Yan and several of his friends, who were also senior physicians, remonstrated that this was not the purpose of medicine or their hospital, which, though small and not well known, had always prided itself on its high clinical standards, rigorous clinical teaching, and applied research directed to health problems salient to the community. The party secretary, Tan Zhiwei, and the director of the hospital, Dr. Wu Zewen, who had formerly worked under Dr. Yan, led a chorus of responses. Dr. Yan, they stated, was a fine clinician and a dedicated teacher and researcher, but he and those who supported his ideas were outdated. China had changed, and greatly so. This was no longer the China of collectivization. This was a new China. The cautions were no long relevant. Did they want the hospital to go the way of other state enterprises that failed to modernize? That way would lead to fiscal crisis, breakdown of the organization, and loss of jobs and retirement benefits. It was good to hear the old ideals reaffirmed, but they were, alas, the values of a time gone by. Dr. Yan noticed that Weiqing remained silent throughout the discussion, which surprised him because Weiqing now headed one of the hospital's major centers and therefore ought to have shared Dr. Yan's concerns and been on his side.

It turned out that Weiqing, Dr. Yan's nemesis, was engaged in even more ambitious planning for re-creating the hospital as an engine of profit making. Over the next several months, Weiqing together with Secretary Tan and Director Wu made public plans to develop property that belonged to the work unit but was a few blocks away into a shopping complex that included restaurants, a hotel, stores, and commercial offices. Indeed, they had already made the initial investments and had lined up a Hong Kong developer and high-level governmental backing. The proposed shopping arcade was particularly difficult for Dr. Yan and his circle to accept because it would replace a rehabilitation unit, a nursing home, and a hostel for the families of patients. The implications of these plans for Dr. Yan and his circle was that the future development of the hospital would be toward highly commercial interests that would undermine the hospital's professional values and academic traditions, remaking its ethos in a direction they could not accept. They complained, but to no avail. This time the administrators and their allies in the city government warned them to mind their own business or suffer the consequences. Years later, Dr. Yan bitterly observed:

"We . . . capitulated. There was no alternative. All of a sudden the operative issues were different. We had in fact become more or less irrelevant, as Director Wu had pointed out. But Mr. Tan was worse. A coarse, hard former military cadre, he shouted at us, if we got in the way he would crush us. We could forget about bonuses or improved retirement benefits. He even threatened to take away our housing. He was like a thug. He knew little about patient care and had little interest in research. His background was in management in the military hospital system. For him our hospital's research tradition and its reputation for strong primary care programs meant nothing. Only the high-tech sector made business sense to him. We could have been a factory for clothes or a department store as far as he was concerned."

According to Dr. Yan, there was general suspicion that the Hong Kong developers had paid off the hospital's leaders. The rumors of corruption deepened when the hotel opened and it became clear that it was not only catering to legitimate guests but also attracting prostitutes and gamblers. "I don't think they were selling illicit drugs," commented Dr. Yan with raised eyebrows, "but that was all they weren't selling. I felt demoralized, as did others. What could have been worse than watching the hospital's investments foster STDs and for all I know HIV/AIDS? That was when I knew I had to get out. I thought I had wasted my career. I became despondent. I once even thought of suicide. Oh, not seriously, but I did have the passing idea that it would be one form of protest they would have to take seriously." Traditionally in China, the suicide of a high official as a moral protest had to be responded to by the emperor and had great cultural significance for ordinary people.

At this low point, Weiqing approached Dr. Yan and began in a sympathetic voice by telling Dr. Yan that soon both of them would need to retire. Things were moving so fast in medicine that their generation was outdated. What China needed anyway was not strong practitioners but strong researchers who would bring China up to speed on the huge development of biotechnology that was shaking medicine worldwide. Weiqing said there was potentially a huge amount of money to be made in biotechnology. Look at the United States, he said; everyone there was getting in on biotech. Pretty soon China would develop such companies, and it was precisely the moment to form one of them. What the hospital needed to do was to spin off a private firm, attract a large amount of capital from Hong Kong and Singapore, and hire researchers, especially Chinese who were returned students from the United States or who could be lured back from the States. They could cater to the problems of wealthy overseas Chinese, Weiqing enthused, and develop new drugs for problems such as impotence, baldness, infertility, depression, and obesity. They could apply for foreign grants for some of the work, and maybe global pharmaceutical companies could be joint partners, he continued. Then Weiqing came to the point. What they needed was a front man, someone credible and with a background that spanned research and clinical practice. Someone who could speak before audiences, meet with investors, inspire researchers, and represent the company internationally. Dr. Yan had good English, had contacts in Hong Kong through his family, was a scientist and a clinician, and was the right age to run the company. As Dr. Yan recalled, Weiqing concluded, "Don't worry—Tan, Wu and I will work behind the scenes on the business side of things. You will only represent us. Lots of people here admire you even if you're not that well known at the national level. But you will be in the future. You could make a lot of money and become famous too. Think about it."

"Everything Weiqing said blackened my heart. I felt as if a large stone sat cold and hard in my stomach," Dr. Yan reported. After taking a few moments to calm his emotions, Dr. Yan accused Xu Weiqing of being a scoundrel, ready to do anything and everything to advance his own ambitions without a thought for others or for the best interests of the institution they had worked in for decades. But even as he spoke

the words, Dr. Yan knew he was defeated. Weiqing had everything working in his favor. The time was ripe. The idea
was logical and attractive. The administrators were fully behind it. It would change the hospital completely, but who
could say it wouldn't succeed? If it did, the economic condition of everyone in the work unit might benefit. "I had to face
the truth. What he proposed did represent the future. What I
stood for represented a past that perhaps could not be re-
vived again. I stopped, not completing my thoughts. I had
nothing to say." Dr. Yan said he was amazed at what Weiqing
said next, not because of its content but because Weiqing was
so brazen. He called Dr. Yan blind, telling him that he had
never figured out that in China you need first of all to find
out which way the wind is blowing and go in that direction
without hesitating and before others passed you by. "'Do what
you need to do to get ahead,' Xu told me. 'Before it was
ultraleftism, so you ran left. Now it's capitalism, so you run
right. Even the police and army are into it in a big way. Stand
still, and you lose out. Stand up and try to obstruct the force
of change and you are lost. The only thing that matters is to
get ahead. I'm stuck with this lousy hospital. It was never big
enough or famous enough for my ambition. But still, it's what
I have. Otherwise, I would have jumped into the sea long ago
and become an entrepreneur. Now biotechnology plus the
shopping plaza is all we have to get ahead. We need to become more capitalist than the capitalists, more crooked than
the crooks. This society is run by thugs. You know it as well
as I do, but you never came to terms with what that means
for our lives. I figured it out long ago. They screwed me and
you and everyone else. They made me do the things I've had

to do to survive. Be hard, very hard. That's what I've learned over all these years.'

"Then," Dr. Yan remarked, "he turned on me and said he would be hard on me. He told me to get out, get out now, if I couldn't accept the offer. There would be no room for me. 'Go to your daughter in America,' he shouted. I felt like slapping him in the face. But all my pent-up anger at Weiqing quickly dissipated. I felt numb all over. It was the end. There really was no more to say. I never spoke to him again, even at my retirement party, just before I departed for America.

"Why did I leave, you ask? Well, Weiqing was right. It was time to retire. I couldn't do much for the hospital. I didn't want to be a mere figurehead and used like a puppet. I hear that Weiqing has started up the biotech firm and that he is the head. Maybe that's what he wanted all along. I feel like one of the traditional scholars of ancient times. I've retreated to a remote place to be a recluse." In Chinese history, when the scholar-bureaucrats who administered the country under the emperor lived through a period of dynastic change or other times of turmoil when they felt the moral context was unacceptable, they could try to refuse high office and administrative responsibilities by becoming recluses, feigning madness, or simply retiring. While this did not always save them, it was taken as a sign of their criticism and protest against a particular time and leadership. "Perhaps it's my way of surviving. I can remember the past as if it were here right now, but I have no sense of what the future will be like. My feelings and values belong to the past. Even in the worst days I could still sense that I knew what I should do. Now I'm very unclear. What once was good is now bad; what once was bad is now good. And still we live on. Some days I feel dizzy, as if I couldn't find my place on the ground. It's not the same ground. What matters now doesn't appeal to me, and, having finally gotten out of China, it doesn't have to appeal to me. America will never be my home either. But I'm with my daughter and we have each other. My sons are doing well. The grandchildren might come to America someday. Who knows, maybe we will someday return to China."

Yan Zhongshu's story is the story of modern China beginning in the 1930s. Huge societal transformations—wars, political revolution, social turmoil—overwhelmed Dr. Yan's hospital, his family, and his own personhood. What happens to ordinary experience as politics and the economy refashion moral life is clear here to a degree not often visible in societies where change is much slower and not nearly so decisive, and where outcomes are more complex and multiform. The close connection between emotion and values is also clear in the instances of Dr. Yan's narrative of angry betrayal, loss of face, and terrified acquiescence to mass violence. Dr. Yan's experiences in a society that is politically oppressive and socially tumultuous, and which morally has undergone an about-face in public values and even in private life, demonstrate how transient human conditions are and how mistaken it is to claim an essential human nature that is beyond history and culture. How to live a moral life amidst such dangers and uncertainty is an unresolved but pressing question for Dr. Yan and for many other Chinese. Moral experience for them connects the public domain of contested meanings and power to the innermost world of sensibility, and it does so in an unpredictable way, as Dr.

Yan's visceral inability to extract revenge from his nemesis, Dr. Xu, so dramatically illustrates.

How best to understand Dr. Yan, Dr. Xu, and their opposite reactions to the precarious political climate in which they were both forced to live? Distinct patterns of action mark their personalities like different signatures. Dr. Xu's deep cynicism and sociopathic disregard for others and his willingness to succeed at any cost, including persistent deceit and betrayal, all carried out without lasting remorse or regret, mark him as dangerously unethical. The fact that Dr. Yan also survived with entirely different behaviors undermines Dr. Xu's self-exculpatory defense that in bad times you have to do bad things to survive. And yet Dr. Yan, for all his idealism and criticism of collaboration, also recognizes that survival in the local worlds torn apart by radical Maoism required keeping these critical self-reflections hidden. In his own way, Dr. Yan was also a collaborator; he had to be to live in the most dangerous times. At the few points at which he overtly resisted the vector of political force (resisting revenge and turning down being a figurehead), it was possible to do so, and he knows that. Even his story, as framed for me, an interested foreigner, is a kind of survival strategy, keeping his self-image (and mine of him) unsullied, agentic, and open to new and different possibilities in a new and different world. Dr. Yan's moral authority itself is based in framing his biography as a moral tale of resisting corruption and hypocrisy. He is already bringing an external ethics to bear on the radical shifts of local moral experience. There is no hero here. And while Dr. Xu's commitment to do all that it takes to maximize his personal advantage as what matters most comes to seem appalling, he is no monster either. His betrayals and the self-serving cynicism of his final speech may damn him for the reader, but it is actually Dr. Xu, not Dr. Yan, who saves the hospital, admittedly by distorting its mission, and who remains in China contributing to its development and his survival. Rather than a stark story of good versus evil, Dr. Yan's account speaks to the gray zone of survival, the banality of moral compromise leading to untoward outcomes, and the unmasterable features of moral life.

Dr. Yan becomes more accepting of his family's modus vivendi, collaboration, although it remains for him a disappointing reality of Chinese society. He told me in one of our final interviews that his family and the thousands like them had little choice, if they wished to survive and do well, but to try to work with local authorities, even if those authorities abused political power. His regret came from his recognition of the downside of this moral climate: collaboration with unethical policies and corrupt practices, continued injustice and inequality, and lost opportunity for reform. It is the irresoluble tension between personal refusal to do the worst and collective willingness to collaborate with lesser evils if need be that disappoint him in the possibilities of leading a moral life. And with a sad and telling realism, he recognizes that it is Dr. Xu, not himself, who can create a viable future for his work unit in the China of today, a China whose current local worlds alienate him thoroughly (perhaps too thoroughly). For Dr. Yan, and for me, Xu's victory is a despairing one. And yet his own defeat—for that is how Dr. Yan sees it, as a defeat—signifies for me the survival of aspiration for something finer and better that remoralizes the world. Dr. Yan's refusal to exile Xu at the hospital's mass meeting breaks the cycle of revenge and serves as an uncanny but greatly important instance of moral imagination and responsibility. He would not go along with violence even when he would benefit, and he found a way to create an unexpected and more promising outcome.

Moral experience has no ending. Ethical reframings, such as the one I propose above, may be used to make it seem that Dr. Yan is the ultimate victor. But I prefer (and I think Dr. Yan himself prefers) to place emphasis on the uncertainty and unfinished character of the struggle to master experience that is unmasterable. Ordinary moral experience is rarely about victories. No human story can use the word *ultimate*. Count no man happy until the end, goes the refrain of the ancient Greek chorus. I take this to mean that in fashioning a moral life we are always subject to limits to what we can control, outcomes we cannot predict, and deep dangers that are ever present. It is not a matter of waiting until Yan Zhongshu and Xu Weiqing are dead to judge their lives; rather, there is no ultimate basis for comparison. Seen in that light, Dr. Yan looks more antiheroic than anything else. It is, after all, his critical self-reflection on the dangers of the world and the self that open a space, even if a tiny and an unstable one, for protest, resistance, and potential remaking. And that is where my own ethical positioning comes in. I share Dr. Yan's concerns and critiques, but as an outsider who has not had to exist over the long term within China's moral ethos, I am hesitant to judge and advocate something I think is better. Perhaps what Dr. Yan's narrative really tells us is how greatly difficult it is to be alive as a subject in the local world and at the very same time stand back from or otherwise apart from the local so that you can bring into it an extra- or supralocal perspective to evaluate local experience and offer an alternative ethical vision. And yet, as difficult as that balancing act is, that is what needs to happen. If there is to be an ethics that humanly matters, then it must be part of the moral-emotional-political messiness that is what local life is. Dr. Yan's narrative, that is, shows us just how painfully difficult it is to step outside our practical personal and societal responsibilities (our moral world), imagine some other, more availing ways to live, and put them into practice. His story also shows us that coming to terms with the dangers and uncertainties of our lives, however painful and troubling it is to confront what matters, is the existential responsibility we owe our humanity to craft a moral life that is not simply the mechanical reaction of a cog in the machine but reflects the human potential for self-knowledge and collective refashioning of who we are and where we are headed. This is the ethical requirement of human experience—not easy, never fully accomplished, always caught up in the limits of politics, social life, and our own genetically and psychologically based passions, but, at the end, what moral life is for.

5

Charles Kentworth Jamison

I have waited fifteen years to tell this story of pain and the holy; suffering, sex, and redemption; religion and medicine. I met the man I will call Charles Kentworth Jamison, a minister from a liberal Protestant denomination in the Pacific Northwest, in a university hospital's chronic pain clinic, where for several years I was an attending psychiatrist. Following an intensive evaluation, I saw him every few months for two years. After I moved east, we stayed in contact for six years via telephone and letters, and he came to see me on one occasion for a lengthy follow-up interview. A large-bodied, tall (about six foot three), robust man, usually dressed in well-tailored and fashionable but informal attire, with an expressive face and head of thick, unruly white hair, Reverend Jamison was in his sixties when we first met. He had been suffering from severe episodes of pain in his head and neck for at least two decades and had developed a characteristic movement, a kind of tic, that represented his pain. Every few minutes his right hand would massage his neck and the back of his head, while he simultaneously turned them downward and from right to left. The pain was constantly present at a modest level, but periodically—every week or two, it seemed— it would get much, much worse. At those times, Jamison took semieffective non-narcotic pain medication but refused stronger narcotic analgesics, which would have quelled the pain altogether. In order to dampen the pain's intensity to an endurable level, he would stop whatever he was doing, go into his bedroom, pull the shades closed, turn off all the lights, lie flat on the bed, and struggle to make his mind go blank and relax.

Unlike most pain patients I interviewed at the clinic, Jamison had not himself chosen to seek expert help. Instead, he had with great reluctance accepted the strong advice of his doctors and family, who had grown frustrated by his inability to control his chronic pain. Jamison's reason for attending the pain clinic was not the only thing that distinguished him from the other patients. In the course of our first interview, Reverend Jamison shocked me so thoroughly that the routine line of questioning, which focused on the problems pain either created or intensified in the patient's life, and which I had perfected in evaluating hundreds of pain patients, stopped in its tracks.

He looked hard into my eyes and told me all my questions about the negative consequences of pain were entirely off base. As excruciating and debilitating as the pain occasionally was, Jamison saw it as a very good thing. No chronic pain patient I had interviewed had ever confessed to viewing his suffering as beneficial. I blurted out, "Surely, given all that you've been through, you're joking?" He took a deep breath, stroked his head and neck in the characteristic manner, and replied with firm emphasis: "It has caused me to suffer, really suffer. But I still affirm it has been a good, a very good thing."

I asked him to explain what this remark could mean, and Reverend Jamison launched into the following story. He had gone into the ministry in an indirect way, after zigs and zags in his life trajectory. A popular and handsome football hero in high school and college, he had many girlfriends and many sexual affairs during his adolescence and early adulthood. Sex became so urgent in his twenties, he remembers, that he masturbated whenever he was alone while experiencing detailed sexual fantasies that turned on female sexual odors. He became obsessed with these fantasies, so much so that he felt he could do nothing to limit or remove them. The fantasies were so intense and his self-control so weak that he felt unable to subdue them and was, as a result, guilty and ashamed.

In his early thirties he met a remarkable young woman who soon became his wife. Her life experience had been almost the polar opposite of his. Although she was quite beautiful and had a wide circle of friends, she was a virgin and firmly embraced a Protestant abstemiousness equally applied to sex, alcohol, gambling, and frivolity—all of which, except for gambling, were things that Reverend Jamison had delighted in for a decade while he worked as an assistant high school coach and began part-time graduate studies in religion.

At the outset of their marriage, he worked hard to restrain his fantasies and behavior. Their relationship developed into a deep and in his words "miraculous" commitment. As their relationship deepened so did their sexual relationship, becoming more active and mutually joyous. However, five years into that marriage, for no apparent reason, Reverend Jamison found himself experiencing again sexual fantasies of the same intensity as in his early adulthood. He was a graduate student at that time and was surrounded by young women, so he found outlets for his powerful sexual desire. But each time he committed adultery he felt intense guilt, profound unworthiness, and self-hatred. Around the same time, his wife became pregnant with the first of their three sons. During that pregnancy's final trimester, she became dangerously hypertensive. (Many women experience some elevation of their blood pressure during pregnancy owing to fluid retention, hormonal surges, and the enlarging fetus pressing on major blood vessels, but some develop very high blood pressure, which, if untreated, can produce stroke, heart attack, or other serious complications.) Because the condition put the lives of both the unborn child and Jamison's wife at risk, the obstetrician suggested terminating the pregnancy, an option the Jamisons quickly rejected. Reverend Jamison told me that not long after that discussion he found himself alone with a young graduate student with whom he previously had had a brief sexual liaison. He was extremely excited: his heart pumping, his thoughts racing, the erotic fantasies vivid like a motion picture in his mind. Then a powerful and unexpected emotion flooded his sensation. He described it as a sensibility of the holy, a physical feeling he associated with accompanying his parents to prayer sessions when he was a child. During those acts of intense prayer, when he felt himself directly addressing God, he had felt his heart and breathing speed up and a sensation of lightness and buoyancy come over his body as if he were floating in the air. Suddenly he would experience a jerking of his neck and his head would snap up and backward.

This time he felt the rapid heartbeat and breathing, experienced the lightness and sensation of floating in the air, and his neck and head snapped back. He sensed that he was in the presence of the divine. He felt first thrilled and then humiliated by the sinfulness of his thoughts. He asked God to help him to control these intrusive thoughts and help his wife so that her hypertension would come under control so she could give birth to a healthy baby. He parted from the young woman, explaining to her great surprise that he could no longer carry on as before because he had been called by God.

Over the next few weeks all that he prayed for came to be. His wife's blood pressure returned to near normal and his own invasive erotic fantasies ceased. A few days before the baby was born he came to the decision that he would follow what he now interpreted as a call to the ministry, an epiphany that had delivered not only a healthy son but also salvation. His wife was surprised and concerned by his determination to become a minister. She was skeptical of "true believers" and what she derisively called "religious magic," and said she had not pictured her husband and herself so involved with a church. Indeed, she considered herself a nondenominational Protestant who found religious meaning in personal relations and nature, not institutions. Her husband reassured her that what he had in mind was not a fundamentalist commitment but a doctrinally liberal yet personally disciplined Protestantism.

Over time, Jamison became a respected minister with a small but active congregation. He practiced a kind of Protestantism that he associated with highly liberal positions on matters of doctrine and ritual and especially social policy. For example, he advocated against the Vietnam War, for civil rights, for women's rights including abortion rights, and for consecration of women as clergy. He considered himself uniquely skilled at pastoral counseling. "Whenever I had a parishioner or family with problems concerning sexuality, adultery, or for that matter violence and other family tensions, I felt my personal experience had prepared me to be empathic, supportive, and helpful in a practical way." He said that he could understand what combination of inner and outer forces drive people to do what seems irrational, as with the case of adolescent turmoil and suicide. He was sought out by adolescents and youth in trouble and developed a local reputation for drawing them back to religious commitments. His career flourished, as did his family life. Their second and third sons were born, and his relationships with his sons and his wife became the central meaning of his life. His wife also began to develop a part-time career as a real estate agent, which over the years elevated their lifestyle.

A few years into his ministry, Jamison encountered another decisive moment. A young woman who had worked in a professional escort service and as a nude dancer came to see him. She complained of experiencing elaborate erotic fantasies and sometimes acting on them. Reverend Jamison felt himself faltering for the first time in years. "It became clear pretty quickly I wasn't prepared to deal with this. It was way too seductive. On the one side I wanted to help this woman, and on the other side, I wanted to act it out with her. I began to feel out of control myself, and a hypocrite. You know, I'm counseling youngsters who are pushed into sexual activity at an early age by our culture's preoccupation with sex and youth, and on the other hand, I'm experiencing the same biological and psychological urges they are, [and those urges were just] as uncontrollable. . . . I didn't know what to do. One minute my head was full of prayer, the next minute overrun with sex. And I was ready to do it with this poor woman. No, it was worse than that. I called up escort services, then hung up the receiver. I drove my car past X-rated clubs, and part of me wanted to dash in and see and do all kinds of things. I started masturbating again. I was about to dive off the deep end. My own congregation was physically near to a couple of X-rated movie houses and bars with advertisements for live nude dancing. It was a real bad area but one you drove through on the way to shopping. Suppose my church members saw me going into one of these places or were there themselves? How would I deal with it? I felt so torn between desire and guilt I could have screamed. Then my wife had a business trip that took her out of town for several weeks. That time was pure hell for me. I felt like my body had become a battle zone for endlessly conflicting emotions. Terrible."

Then, at a point at which Reverend Jamison felt he could no longer control himself and was about to give into his over-whelming sexual fantasies, he experienced what he would later call "divine intercession." He woke up one morning, after spending the night sleepless and sexually aroused, with a stiffness in his neck and an ache in the back of his head. Over the course of several days the sensation worsened into the pain he experiences today. At first he interpreted the pain literally as God's punishment. Later he took it to be God's grace. Periodically, over the decades, especially at times when he feels a return of fantasies and can (outside of intercourse with his wife) smell sexual scents, the pain worsens into a stronger paroxysm. The intense pain both breaks the intrusiveness of sexual fantasies and produces relief and a sense of control. It follows a trajectory of transformation from the unendurable to the endurable and then to the spiritually transporting. For Jamison, his pain increasingly fused with religious sensibility, enabling him to identify with Jesus on the cross. It became a feeling of transcendence, as if he was moving through suffering to the sublime.

Pain, for Reverend Jamison, is salvational, converting a harmful and unwanted desire into a state of grace and redemption. "You've got to see it my way," he explains. "The pain hurts a lot and periodically disables me, but much more often it empowers me. It has made me much more attuned to the bodily representation of the spiritual and emotional state of others. It has made me a better listener. But more than that, it makes such a powerful difference in my own life.

"I see religion in the body, in emotions, in personal and family struggles. And of course for me, it brings me closer to God. I believe it is my struggle between evil and good, and good wins. It is an experience of the holy born out of the flowers of evil. It teaches me that we are not helpless when powerful desire takes over. It makes me more aware and more critical of how our own culture manipulates desire. It has made me a better minister, especially to youth and adolescents in trouble. I know what they are going through. I be-

lieve religion can be right there with them in their experiences. I've learned, I guess, that for people like me the world
is not so much about moral choice. How could I make a rational choice in the face of overwhelming bodily feelings? Religion is what makes moral life feasible in the face of such
powerful cultural and biological currents. Religion makes the
body remember; pain can be a religious memory. That's why
I can say, honestly say, my pain has been a source of good in
my life. Doctors don't get it. The pain clinic didn't. This is a
religious, not a medical, thing."

Jamison did not use his criticism of cultural and biological
forces shaping experience to justify his own failings, about
which he was equally critical. These forces were not scape-
goats in his way of seeing life. His own failings were his responsibility, he told me repeatedly. Yet these highly personal
problems, he also insisted, could not be controlled or rem-
edied by individuals alone. The confluence of cultural messages, biological impulses, and personal actions that was at
the root of addictions to substances and to sex, Reverend
Jamison said to me, required religious intervention. When he
talked about pain as a religious memory, he meant that pain
was his ethical conscience and that it created in his sensibility
the memory of God's grace working in his life.

Jamison's emphasis on the import of religion is not as extraordinary as it may seem. Of all the rich, technologically advanced countries in the world, America has by far the highest
percentage of people who express a belief in God: more than
90 percent of Americans are religious in this sense. In comparison, in more secular European countries, rates of belief can
fall below 65 percent. Also, about two-thirds of Americans

state in surveys that God has been active in their lives. By this they mean that God has guided decisions and affected outcomes. This is a figure that dwarfs the statistics for Europe. Religion in America centers on personal faith and individual spiritual quest more than theological niceties (although certain core Christian tenets such as the sanctity of life have been politicized and clearly are taken very seriously indeed). For example, Americans define religion as the spiritual aspect of the self, whereas Europeans see religion more broadly in terms of theology, ritual, and the institution of the church itself. For European and Latin American Christians the social gospel of justice seems more alive and important than it is for U.S. Christians, who have in recent decades turned away from social justice toward more individual cultural values such as personal liberation and salvation. William James's *Varieties of Religious Experience,* which defines religion in psychological terms, remains popular a century after its original publication. For James religion was a feature of mind and feeling, not institutions and rituals. Catholicism and Judaism have been Protestantized in America, with greater emphasis on the deep personal roots of religiosity. Pastoral counseling, which relies on a secular quasi-Freudian approach, is an important aspect in the training of American religionists. This is not the case in many other societies. There priests and ministers counsel about issues of doctrine and religious practice; in the United States they may do so as well, but counseling is largely understood to be a psychological education and treatment.

Thus, religion and psychology are closely related in American society. And religion is also present in alternative and complementary medicine; acupuncture and herbalism, for example, are often practiced along with a language of spirituality. Patients are encouraged to meditate and find their spiritual center. Indeed, in an age of simply enormous technological and scientific advances, religion now infiltrates nearly all aspects of American society, including medicine. Pain specialists have long recognized the role of religion as a source of psychosocial support in the clinical management of chronic pain patients, but biomedicine, the legally defined medical profession and its hospitals and research centers, which had a long history of professional hostility to religion, is newly welcoming to religious issues. Medical students are now introduced to religious questions in courses on patient-doctor relations, and medical ethicists, psychiatrists, and primary care physicians are expected to show genuine respect for religious concerns. Today, there is a new rapprochement between religion and biomedical science, with researchers studying how spiritual practices and religious rituals may influence the hormonal system and with it immunological and neurological processes that have physiological effects on infection, pain, the placebo effect, and healing. Stress works through this hormonal system to alter cardiovascular and mental states. Religious practices have been shown to limit or even reverse these effects. Harnessing the healing benefits of religious practice is now a serious scientific undertaking in medicine.

Religionists played a founding role in the development of American bioethics. Religious values are often of concern to patients and families and caregivers at the end of life and in other serious clinical scenarios. Reverend Jamison was involved in psychological counseling. He was deeply interested in the science of stress and how religious practice affected stress responses, including his own. He worked with ethicists on clinical issues, including those around the end of life. And he was fascinated by religious healing. But I am especially interested in the religious entanglement with moral experience in his life, illness, and treatment.

Reverend Jamison's everyday bodily experience, in his perspective, becomes a personal battleground between good and evil, desire and divinity. God's grace, he believes, keeps him from succumbing to sexual impulses that earlier he acted on in ways that made him feel sinful. Pain mediates between his intimate struggles and the holy. Pain is salvific, saving him from the torments and humiliation of desires he can otherwise not control. Pain orders his experience, not only signaling what matters most but realizing it. And it prepares him, in his mind, for his ministry, which seeks out those who, like himself, suffer from powerful psychological processes they cannot master.

I am most definitely not implying here that all physical suffering is the result of God's will. I am reporting what Reverend Jamison said throughout the years I knew him. For Jamison, leading a moral life amidst danger and uncertainty that matched his ethical aspirations meant living with pain and finding God through that pain. Suffering had for him positive ethical significance that transcended medical diagnosis and treatment. Pain is part of moral life, he insisted, and it remade his way of living so that he could surmount the chief moral peril he faced.

Of course I have worked with other patients for whom religion loomed on the other side of the pain equation, including ministers and their spouses whose pain was worsened by their ministries, including their extensive social obligations. For example, one rural minister's spouse's back pain intensified when the large social obligations she had in their rural community made her feel trapped in a glass bowl where she could not express herself. Many people who experience pain do not interpret their suffering in religious terms. I have sat by the bedside of patients whose severe episodes of pain could not be controlled by prayer and who felt nothing at all in the way of religious transformation. Their moral worlds and bodily habitus were quite different from that of Reverend Jamison. Several felt that God had abandoned them. Others observed that pain itself was the main danger in their lives. Several chronic pain patients told me that to control the severity of the symptoms, they had shut down their careers and family, and their way of living had been greatly impoverished.

Reverend Jamison refers to the body in pain as a source of memory. The body remembers the unsuccessful struggles to master unwanted experience, and the suffering body remembers God. Embodiment—namely, experiencing meaning through bodily process, such as pain—is a means of collective as well as individual memory. As numerous researchers have noted, bodily practices such as a certain pattern of gestures, movements, body piercing, or physical complaints can represent cultural meanings and social position. In this case, embodiment unites emotions, values, and ritual. Reverend Jamison's bodily tic can be interpreted as the outward expression of an internalized prayer, a ritual of remembrance, a religious practice calling forth the presence of divinity. The efficacy of his prayer is not found in the disappearance of his pain, as it so often is in healing rituals; rather, the pain itself, as it is made over into the sacred, is the source of his moral triumph in sublimating unwanted sexual desires into religious meaning. Perhaps in this way, Reverend Jamison's experience comes close to early Christian and medieval representations of pain as sacred in itself, an aspect of the suffering self that acts as a mediating bridge between the person and God. The point has been made by historians of Christianity that early Christians valued a suffering self in contrast to Roman stoicism's devaluing of suffering. For Christians, the suffering self linked their experience of the world with Christ's. Suffering itself was valued for this religious reason. Jamison's illness narrative too is not about an easy or superficial healing, or even healing at all.

Of course, there is also a more skeptical reading of the reverend's tale. Some might read into it indiscipline, absence of self-control, immature sexual desire, and the abuse of religion as a merely utilitarian device to cover over a deeply problematic ethical failing. This is not how I personally saw Reverend Jamison nor continue to imagine his inner world, but I cannot contest an alternative perspective. Perhaps for some Reverend Jamison is sinful, a self-deceiving preacher, unworthy of ministering to others with his own inner world in such disarray. This core tension between different readings of Reverend Jamison's story—pain as authenticity versus pain as deception—reflects a deep current of uncertainty and suspicion in human conditions of chronic pain. Is the pain that authorizes disability benefit claims real or is it a strategic ploy (conscious or unconscious) to obtain financial support, among other benefits? This core conundrum in chronic pain care challenges a naive therapeutic understanding as a mis-representation of a deeper, more disturbing reality. Because moral experience involves strategic acts meant to alter the perspectives of others, our ethical reflections can be taken to be disingenuous moves in games of power. We use pain for local purposes. Viewed this way, Reverend Jamison could be regarded as a sociopath, with religion merely camouflage for antisocial behavior.

As I have framed the issues in the preceding chapters, Reverend Jamison's local world must be the starting point for understanding his pain experience. But then what? Do we follow Emmanuel Lévinas's insistence that face-to-face acknowledgment of his suffering is the basic ethical action? Lévinas holds that ethics always comes first, and ethics means affirming other persons and their suffering. But what if this suffering is inauthentic? And if so, where does that leave his caregivers and family, who experienced such frustration? So what should be the ethical response to Jamison's perplexing moral experience? Is the core ethical action one of criticizing the reverend's too comfortable and comforting dilemma followed by pressure to get him to give up his painful yet accommodating defense in favor of some less costly (to family and health care providers) way of coming to terms with his biography and his passion? Is the change that is called for not within his psyche but in his world—that is, in his relationships with his wife, children, and parishioners? Or does the problem lie in the inadequacy of ethics itself to come to terms with Jamison's unsettling emotional and moral turmoil? This range of questions might have helped me shape a therapeutic response better than administration of yet another pain questionnaire or newly developed analgesic. In the care of patients with chronic pain and other chronic illnesses, professional and family caregivers need to address the ethical and religious issues as much as the medical and psychological ones.

In the end, I guess I intuitively followed Lévinas's model. I affirmed Reverend Jamison's experience of pain as well as his religious experience as real. And I dealt with his sexual fantasies not just as a psychological problem but as a moral one. But I wondered about the alternative. For as we shall encounter it in a later chapter's description of the contributions of W. H. R. Rivers, medical intervention turns not only on the relation between moral experience and emotions but also on the politics of everyday life. It is the latter—the political side of family and work experience—that seems least developed in my interpretation. What was religiously transformative for Reverend Jamison was pure frustration for his wife, children, parishioners, and doctors. Was his the politics of resistance against the conventional constraints of the everyday middle-class American world? Did his chronic pain experience provide Reverend Jamison with sanction for his criticism of the dangerous effects of American society on adolescent and young adult sexual development and their handling of violent impulses? Did his religious response to his pain legitimate his countercultural therapeutic efforts on their behalf, including his insistence that what medical professionals and increasingly laypersons regarded to be the individual pathologies of adolescents in turmoil requiring medical treatment was in fact conflict and contradiction in Americans' moral experience over sex and substances—cultural conflict and contradiction requiring ethical and ultimately religious intervention? Did this apply to his own personal encounter with chronic pain, pain that defeated his caregivers, including the medical system? Not having carried out an ethnography of Reverend Jamison's local world, I can't answer these questions with any conviction. But over the years, my encounter with Reverend Jamison and many other patients whose chronic pain frustrated professional medical and family caregivers has only intensified this line of inquiry. Pain changed their world. On superficial psychological and medical reckoning these changes seemed entirely negative. But applying broader social interpretation, I have often wondered, as in the case of Winthrop Cohen, if bodily experience of pain, depression, exhaustion, and other chronic symptoms are not alternative forms of criticism and protest, and, in the case of Reverend Jamison, action meant to have societal effects making over local worlds into new moral conditions.

What I mean here is that once such symptoms have become chronic, for whatever biological or psychological reason, they can also come to express, say, the alienation that a patient feels from society, criticism of a spousal relationship or that with a business supervisor or co-worker, or protest against financial and political realities more generally. Chronic pain is a major complaint for the American disability system, and because so many of those who receive disability benefits are working-class or poor, that system is sometimes regarded as an indirect transfer of wealth in a society characterized by increasing social and economic inequalities without many other means of transferring resources. Thus, chronic pain, in this regard, could also be viewed as a weapon of the weak, an action meant to improve economic and social conditions. As I noted in Dr. Yan's story, during the collective trauma of China's Cultural Revolution many intellectuals and cadres who became political targets developed symptoms of neurasthenia. Three of these—headache, dizziness, and severe fatigue—seemed to express collective as well as personal feelings of exhaustion with the political campaigns, disorientation in a society in which the leaders and even the values were being overturned, and pain from the trauma of public criticism. Under the repressive political regime of the People's Republic of China, this was one of the few ways to express protest and criticism. For Reverend Jamison pain was not just a complaint but a way of coping with the frustrations of a cultural gap between actually lived moral values and expressed ethical aspirations that he took to be a huge and dangerous hypocrisy, a hypocrisy that he recognized in himself as well. And through his actions on behalf of troubled youth, Reverend Jamison could be viewed as acting on his own world to reduce that gap between the real and the ideal out of a religious passion whose source seemed to be the pain of unacceptable sexual desires. In that sense, we might imagine Reverend Jamison going beyond criticism and protest of American culture to try to remake the psychocultural dynamics of youth inhabiting his world. Whether or not we agree with this interpretation of pain, we can still appreciate that for Reverend Jamison there is an ethical project of transforming the self and the world.

6

Sally Williams

For those who are seriously sick and for those who care for them, illness is quintessentially moral. Serious illness elicits the deepest and most complex emotions: fear and demoralization, rage and humiliation, but also the awareness of previously unrecognized values. Illness can, for some, make life matter. A newly diagnosed cancer patient, for example, has had to work through the anguish of uncertain diagnostic tests. There is also a limbo-like state in which emotions swirl between expectations of polar opposites, normality and death, before she is told she definitely has cancer. During the trials of treatment, denial can alternate with giving up. Along the trajectory of cancer care, she concentrates her focus on completing the treatment, but also on those people and things that matter now. She may rediscover her religious connections, revivify her marriage, find that neighbors really can help, sink into such despair that for the first time in her life she is willing to do psychotherapy, or reconnect with elderly parents to talk through family burdens she never thought she could voice. I have interviewed such patients, as well as many others who felt with a new limit placed on their days they would do those things that brought beauty, happiness, and hope: travel, return to long-dormant artistic interests, read, learn a new sport, buy clothes, pray. If the cancer can't be controlled, this woman's end-of-life days will turn on moral meanings, from the way she seeks to die to the rituals and ceremonies she wishes to memorialize her life and all the business of ending life—wills, funeral arrangements, confession, final words—that few can imagine is truly final until we actually do it. Examining the cultural and personal nexus of illness is another way of understanding what really matters.

Sally Williams is a fifty-four-year-old artist and owner of a small art gallery in New York City. Tall, dark-haired, round-faced, her olive skin tanned and glowing, she looks a decade younger. Sally's gaze is open and direct, and yet there is something in her visage—"a shade of sadness, a blush of shame," in John Greenleaf Whittier's words—that gathers darkness and suggests things deeper and hidden, hurtful things. In her adulthood Sally has been many things—the daughter of a depressed, alcoholic father and a mother with advanced Alzheimer's dementia; a wife who has been separated from and reconnected with her husband, Daniel, a business consultant and environmentalist, and their three adult children; a talented landscape painter whose work has been displayed in galleries and purchased by museums; a successful small-business owner with a thriving gallery; a member of a small, closely knit network of friends, most of whom are artists and writers; and, most tellingly, a recovered drug addict who two years before I first interviewed her was diagnosed with AIDS. I have known Sally's husband for two decades out of a mutual interest in things Chinese; I got to know Sally slightly through him. After she found out about her diagnosis she asked me if I would be interested in interviewing her because of my research with patients suffering chronic diseases. I had done something like this with patients with other disorders on several occasions. Sally and I have had eight interviews stretched out over five years.

When Sally first discovered she was infected, in 1997, she was completely straightforward and open about her disease: "I wanted my children, each of them, to know my AIDS status, and my friends too." Sally reports it wasn't easy telling them, or her husband, but when she finished she felt "liberated." It was particularly hard "to explain all that I did for two truly miserable, horrific years, after the separation from my husband Daniel, a decade ago. I became a dope addict, about as low as you can get, doing anything for a fix. That's when I got infected, though I didn't know it until two years ago, when I developed chronic diarrhea and exhaustion."

Sally looked back over the eight years between when she got clean and when she discovered she had AIDS: "You see, I had spent those years building myself back up again. I made a good place in the world. I became a successful artist and an effective businesswoman. I made the gallery into something special, and then that bad time came back in the worst way to haunt me, to hurt me. AIDS. I felt ashamed all over again. I had stayed clean. But I wasn't clean of infection. I learned I had AIDS at what was turning out to be the very best time of my life."

Sally continued: "I wish I could say I've managed well. I've had big ups and downs since learning I was infected. Two of my kids, my boys, at first turned away from me. They had had enough and were in denial. Now they are supportive and loving. My daughter, Jennifer, God bless her, in spite of all she has to do in graduate school, was there, completely there for me. Most remarkable of all, my husband returned. He came back in my life, back to help. Isn't that crazy! Almost a decade before, he walked out, away from me. He found someone else. I fell apart totally. When I was doing drugs, I actually tried to burn him, to make him pay. . . . Then after two years at rock bottom I rebuilt my life. On my own and starting at the bottom, I succeeded . . . in my art, in my business, and in my . . . well, in the art of living. So then I get seriously sick with this terrible disease and he comes back. A different man, a different me, and a different, a very different relationship. He is . . . well, great. We still don't live together, yet we might as well. He is always here with me. He wants to take care of me, and he does. He takes care of me. We are deeply, fully in love again."

Sally's marriage is not the only aspect of her life that has stabilized. She has experienced two serious opportunistic infections that could have killed her. "They knocked me to my knees. Terrible! I was completely out of it; thought I was on the way out." But now she takes twenty pills each day and is symptom-free, looking healthy and flourishing. "It is incredible, how these pills make this disease a chronic condition you can live with. Imagine if I had AIDS at the outset of the epidemic with nothing to stop the progression . . . dying slowly, day by day, in pain, with diapers, nothing but skin and bones, demented, vomiting, shitting, and with so much ignorance and stigma like a dark halo encasing me."

Previously a reticent, self-involved, deeply private woman, Sally astonishes herself by her newfound outspokenness and activism on behalf of AIDS and drug abuse programs. Sally is explicit about this change in her personhood: "Something snapped. Something gave way . . . some deep hesitance. I feel a new Sally Williams. Less, much less self-absorbed; more, much more out there . . . saying what needs to be said. I've got no time now for indirection. I speak up, speak out, and it's not about me. I kinda lose my sense of self in some much larger, more important world out there."

This appealing image of becoming absorbed in something larger, something in which you lose the self, recurs throughout our talks. Sally is convinced that enlisting in the AIDS and drug abuse movements is a positive transformation in who she is. She overcomes a formerly compelling privacy and moves beyond an inhibiting selfishness toward action in the world, action on behalf of others. The sense of inner resistance giving way so that she can do things means that whatever held in check her ability to engage with others also limited her own artistic and business talents. Traveling inward inhibited her; traveling outward into the larger world is liberating. She experiences creativity and happiness, in spite of her serious sickness, and she does so by losing the self, and its inhibiting preoccupations, in doing things that matter to her now.

"I feel an inner pressure to make my ideas known and to do something about them. Act on them." Without trying to excuse or defend herself, Sally refers to her pre-drug-abuse and pre-AIDS persona as a "taker." She explains: "I was so selfish that, looking back, I realize I was caught up in what I could get out of people, even the family. I was not a giver. I took and I expected more. I simply didn't concentrate [on] what I could do for others. Not a good way to be, but I've got to be honest, that's the way I was."

Despite her previous self-absorption, Sally feels that she's "different now. I really am. I see beyond, well beyond me. I guess I realize that when I die, and who knows how soon that will be, I'll . . . well, I'll be taken up in the immensity of the universe. What remains won't be me, but what I've done for others. This damn disease, and actually also the drug abuse, is my great teacher. Life is about doing for others—family, friends, the world, I guess. I've got no time for my inner demons. They're not important enough. I'm not important enough. I'm here to get on with it, get on with the big things that count, that count for me and, more importantly, for others. . . .

"I know now that we are in the middle of a great plague, a world epidemic like the Black Death in the Middle Ages, and we are mostly oblivious to it. Actually there are two epidemics, deadly ones: AIDS and drug abuse. And they go together, as I know from a hard, hard experience. But because these epidemics are primarily with the poor, with people of color who are made to count for less, we don't do what needs to be done. We don't pour in the resources. We just let this fire burn slowly, consuming those who matter less, until it touches on the world we know, the comfortable, privileged world. . . . Well, I know what these things *are,* from the inside. They changed my life. I want people to wake up.

"Life is one helluva serious business. It hurts you; it can kill you. I was raised like so many people in the U.S., with an entirely false sense of comfort and security. I know! I fell right out of the middle class to the lowest. I sold my body for a fix. I needed drugs so bad I allowed myself to live in filth in a basement with other dope fiends. I shared needles with drugged-out people I hardly knew. We used dirty syringes, dirty water. We were animals. We acted like that because we couldn't control our need, our desire for drugs."

Not unlike Reverend Jamison, Sally Williams contends there are two sources of her tragedy. She acknowledges her own self-ishness as the cause of her self-destructive actions. Yet that failure to feel anything beyond the self as truly valuable she attributes to more than an isolated character flaw. Her selfishness, she argues, is powerfully conditioned by hyperindividualism, narcissism, blindness to the unjust human conditions surrounding us, and deafness to the call from our local world to do something to remedy and repair those inhuman conditions. These are dangerous cultural forces of our time and place that translate into self-destructive (which also means world-destructive) behavior. That is what makes her ashamed of her past, and that is also what makes her feel that, while her past is behind her, she must respond to the call for responsible action.

"Been there, done that!" she concluded emphatically. She continued bitterly: "Oh, I can't even think about it without wanting to cry, to scream. How did I do it? How did I get there? You want to know what I think? I don't mean to offer an excuse, just understand what happened.

"I must have been eleven or twelve when my father started abusing me. It was never sexual. But when he was flat-out drunk—like a couple of times each month—he could be very mean and violent. He punched my mother, made her cry. He slapped me and my brother. Rarely he threw us around, like rag dolls. One night he was a monster, the next day he cried and begged our forgiveness. Most often, he acted, we all acted, like nothing was happening. We weren't supposed to talk about it. No, that's not strong enough: we couldn't, not a word, talk about it. It was like there were two worlds. One up, one upside down. And you couldn't say anything. . . . Well, it made everything seem false, a great pretense of normality covering over a real hell. It was the silence, the secret that came to be the worst part. It eroded all the good, the love, the relationships. It felt dirty and wrong, completely so. It forced me to be suspicious of everything, of everyone. I didn't believe anything that sounded good. I couldn't conceive of actions that could be good. It was like rot warping the structure of our lives as a family and my life." Sally identifies feelings of inexpressible rage, shame, and fear with this formative time in her life. These are the "inner demons" that she associates with being "a taker," being trapped in isolating cycles of hesitancy, self-absorption, and alienation.

"I think it kept going inside me, years and years afterward. Most of the time I guess I was okay. Popular. Attractive. Happy, even. Then periodically I would fall into a dark, dark place. I was angry and depressed. *Hopeless* is not too strong a word. Then, after a spell, I'd climb out of it, back up into my other persona. A few episodes in my marriage, then my husband had enough. He left me when he finally couldn't take it any longer. And that was when . . . oh, God! . . . that was when I . . . I really, totally, absolutely lost it. First I started drinking—a bottle of wine, then stronger things. . . . I knew I was in free fall, like Alice falling into Wonderland, only I was in hell, Dante's circles, falling from one down to the next, until, well, until I . . . I hit the bottom."

She continued with a mixture of anger and sad vulnerability: "I lost control. I lost my identity. I even lost my sense of time and place. I OD'd a couple of times. I got an abscess in my thigh from shooting up with dirty water. Pus oozing out of a hot and swollen mass—painful and ugly. An apt metaphor for my life. I also was hospitalized with hepatitis A. I was suicidal. The more I force myself to think on it, the more I reckon I was thoroughly depressed, all the time. I tried to kill myself twice, once with an OD, the other time with poison. Now it all looks so distant, like another country. Only every time I revisit it, I feel an equal mixture of horror and shame."

Sally told me on several occasions that the depression and suicide attempts represent an alienated, destructive self that had lost its moorings in her world. As she spun out of that world into its predatory margins of drug abuse, prostitution, and the degradations of utter poverty, it was as if she had entered another local world—a "hell" of emotional, economic, and moral inversion, "another country" that now feels horrifying and shameful.

I asked Sally how she got out of it.

"That I really truly don't know. I only know one day I literally pulled myself off the floor. Said that's enough. No more! No more abuse . . . [of] my body, me. I entered a detox program, and I came out clean. One of the less than 10 percent that make it." (Fewer than 10 percent of heroin addicts who enter rehabilitation programs complete those programs and stay clean.)

Soon after she got out of rehab, Sally started painting again. She knew that she had the training and the talent, but she also knew she had to work hard and long at it, something she had never done. "I poured myself into the work. I spent all day absorbed in painting. I woke in the middle of the night and felt a pressure to paint. At first, my work was simply raw energy, emotional hurt, exposed, but after a while it got more mature. I could work things through, difficult things, horrible things. My landscapes got darker, rougher . . . lots of clotted space, dense, viscous space. The colors seemed to come out of some hidden place in me.

"Earlier, when I was painting I never felt like I was a serious artist. I had friends who were, yet it wasn't there for me. I mean, the passion and the need were there, but not the . . . the coming together of inner vision, feeling, and execution. I mean form and sensibility, imagination and experience. Earlier on, I didn't get it, I didn't realize what it was that wasn't happening, only that I seemed to be pretending. I couldn't find, locate the place I wanted to be. It was a great frustration.

"And come to think about it, I felt frustrated with my friends and family too. I mean with how I was with them. With my artist and writer friends, I was a good listener. I supported them. But I really didn't hear what they were struggling to do. I was all on the surface. The ones I admired, why, they were at another level. They seemed to know what mattered, and I was completely unsure. That's what I mean when I say I didn't get it. Kinda the same with Daniel and the children. I loved them fiercely, but I didn't know [how] to show it. I was too self-centered. It was all about me and my feelings of uncertainty. No, I think *inauthenticity* is the right word. I wasn't sure who I was. I wanted to be different with them but I was all encased in myself. Clotted . . .

"After I got back on my feet something happened. I felt this great sense of responsibility, but it wasn't to self-actualize; it was more creating a new way of relating to my friends and family and my work. I was just as serious about them all. That's why the combination of my own art and running the gallery seemed right. I also watched the constraints, or really restraints, that had tied me up in knots, give way, and something new come forward. I felt . . . well, different. More able to be open. More in need of being direct. More willing to risk what it takes to bring all the crazy aspects of my world together. I earlier lacked . . . the strength of conviction to be openly critical. I hadn't been able to act on things, to change them. I let others do the advocacy. I stayed away, I shied away from . . . from, well, power, from influencing others.

"I also had a couple of good breaks with my art. No, I *made* those breaks. I made sure I got reviewed, noticed. It was thrilling and life-affirming to be praised. I realized I had the power to be praised. Nothing like that happened before. I made money. I used it to buy this small place and fill it with paintings from people I [had] known for a long time, people like me. Not big reputations, no famous names. Just damn fine painters. And this place was a success too . . . unbelievable, really. So I had made it back. And it was on my own, on my own terms. That mattered a lot. I had done it. I was doing it.

"Then I found out I had AIDS. Wow, that was a big one! Like I had been hit in the face, pushed against a wall, smashed.

Amazingly, this time no falling down, no giving up. I guess I knew, really knew from the worst experience, what could happen if I let myself fall down. I had been through all that. No more! No, I just couldn't go through it—the loss and the shame—again. I had to work this thing through. Stand up to it. Face who I was and what was happening, what had happened to *me*.

"By then my mother had dementia. Was lost in it. She couldn't even recognize me at first. It was so sad. But I sat with her and gently told her about the AIDS. I don't think she understood much. Yet talking to her made me see things much more clearly. The whole picture. I went on for hours and hours. She would smile at me like I was talking about how to make a pie or how things were in the houses we had lived in. She wasn't there cognitively. Emotionally somehow she seemed to know. She seemed to bless me. . . .

"My father was drinking as usual, but from a bad drunk he has become a sad drunk. He falls asleep. He spins stories. He lets himself show the hurt and despair. I talked to him too. And he kissed me and said he would stick by me, just like I had stuck by him.

"My sons. What can I say? They, like my husband, had been badly burned when I was on drugs. They couldn't handle bad news. Charlie, the oldest, he told me I got what I deserved. He shouted at me. Cursed me. Then he cried. I cried. And he held me tight and told me he was ashamed of himself for how he reacted, not me. He was great from there on. Will was different. He was very quiet. Said almost nothing. Didn't call me back. Didn't return the calls. Dropped out of my life for at least a few months. But then he and his wife, Annie, came around, really came around too. They came over with food, with treats. We have had some great times."

Sally is most regretful about her relationship to her sons. She carries considerable guilt about her parenting, first because she believes she failed to give them all the emotional and practical support they needed when they were young, and second, because during the years of drug abuse she literally dropped out of their lives. Initially when she reappeared she caused even greater pain by exposing them to the desperate life she had "fallen into." Much of her time now is devoted to them and especially to her grandchildren. "I need to be there for them; I know that. That's probably at the top of my priorities, and it's turned out to be wonderful."

Sally's daughter's reaction to the news was quite different from that of her brothers. "Jennifer was great, right from the start. She is a hefty teddy bear of a woman with a big heart. Always was. She held me and helped me. Moved in. Took over. Put school on hold. I think she pulled me through that first week so quickly, so well the rest became easier, much easier. She called [Sally's husband] Daniel. Told him he had to be there, be of use. He came right away. He was practical as usual but seemed distant. He told me how much I had hurt him when I was on drugs, begging for money, shaming him in front of friends. He couldn't trust me then, still wasn't sure he could now. Well, it took maybe a month, and then, miracle of miracles, we were back together. Better than before. We knew what we had now. The other day we went to a cemetery we always admired for its beautiful trees and seaside setting. We bought a plot. Not in a negative, this-is-the-end way. But in a happy, almost giddy, this-is-the-right-thing-to-do, do-now way.

"And my friends have been great too. I knew I had a real circle of friends. Strangely, I had never called on them. When I was doing drugs, I was too ashamed to ask for help. When I started up again, it was me who was doing for them. These last few years, my friends . . . have really been there for me. In the hospital. In the gallery, helping out run the place. Promoting my work. Even helping with the family. Ask Daniel."

Daniel reported that in the two years after she was diagnosed Sally would occasionally explode with rage over her condition. At one time, she kicked a hole in the plasterboard in the bedroom. Another time she smashed a dish on the kitchen tiles. These dramatic outbursts didn't last long. They punctuated much longer periods of gentleness, compassion, and calm. Daniel observed that Sally had long had difficulty handling anger and fear, but that for the most part the AIDS years were better in this regard. In my experience, such eruptions of anger are not uncommon among patients with life-threatening disorders, and also among their caregivers. Sally clearly had held rage in check during the years of physical abuse by her father, and a psychodynamic formulation of her substance abuse, depression, and suicide attempts would have ample evidence for emphasizing anger toward close others and herself. But I did not find anger as crucial an issue for her as the movement from self to world.

"So AIDS has been devastating, no question: a reality check of the most basic kind," Sally observed. "Yet it's also been about something else. In some inexplicable but transporting way, AIDS has taken me to a different place: a place of truth, deep truth, and kindness—love, really."

Sally donates a significant percentage of her earnings to international AIDS treatment and prevention activities as well as to drug treatment programs. She has traveled to Uganda, South Africa, Thailand, and Brazil to visit AIDS and drug abuse programs. She has attended international AIDS conferences and contributed to a global lobbying effort aimed at convincing the major pharmaceutical companies to allow sophisticated AIDS drugs to be made available as low-cost generic medications for poor people in the developing world. Sally has written a short, unpublished memoir of her drug abuse and AIDS experience that she has shared with close friends and family. It is unsentimental and unsparing in its self-criticism.

In her memoir there is much of the sensitive description that one would expect from an artist whose painterly eye picks up on subtle detail and shadings in the rich context of her life. But there is also a single compelling theme that infuses the memoir with a hard-earned philosophy of life. We become who we are, Sally insists, because of the way we engage with the very real dangers in the world. Life-threatening diseases such as AIDS can bring into focus what really matters and can pressure sufferers to create certain changes, not just inside but in the outside world too. In Sally's case such change took place in her subjective self, in her art, in her circle of family and friends, and in the world of policies and programs concerned with drugs and AIDS.

I HAVE HAD MANY clinical and research interviews with AIDS patients as well as with many others suffering from other grave health conditions. Eighteen years ago I published *The*

Illness Narratives, a collection of individual portraits of real people living with severe chronic diseases—cancer, heart disease, depression, diabetes, chronic pain. From my experience, I know that Sally Williams's story is not representative. Much more commonplace are loss, desperation, and failure cascading into bitterness, isolation, and withdrawal. The disabling consequences of the disease pathology and the responsiveness or resistance to treatment are influential here, yet what is most important is the patients' subjective self, the quality of their relationships, and the moral life they imagine that can be fashioned out of pain and adversity.

There is not any single overdetermined meaning to disease; rather, the experience of serious illness offers a means of understanding in a particularly deep and powerful way what personal and collective moral experience is about. It is, to be sure, always various and contradictory, and yet it also illustrates the core existential insight that the things most at stake are clarified, for us and others, by the dangers we encounter. Those dangers, moreover, can and often do remake what matters most, so that what matters and who we are is not what was before, but instead becomes something new and different.

In a state of siege, Sally redefined her life and her world. Sally's optimistic story demonstrates that experiences of life's very real dangers not only are about injury and limitation but also hold the potential of creative and inspiring change. Creative because they open new realities; inspiring because, in the face of pain and death, these experiences change intimate others, offering the possibility that their moral life can also be different. In Sally's case, her experience with disease led her to open her eyes to the greater world out there, and to hear its call for us to respond to what really matters to others.

Middle-class American society often tries to blind itself to the problems of crime, violence, drug abuse, and AIDS and attributes these problems to those who have fallen out of the circle of wealth, happiness, and hope. Sally's own fall from grace made her deeply suspicious of gates, walls, and separate worlds, domestic or public. She insists that AIDS and drug abuse, and also poverty and violence and stigma, must be seen as part of all of our worlds. Only this way can we overcome silence and denial and get on with the struggle to deal effectively with human misery and its sources. In her view, there is no place to hide. There can be no completely secure domain, safe from the dangers that beset most people.

Serious disease can do that to people. It can open eyes, break down doors, encourage active engagement with real threats and their societal causes. That it most frequently doesn't have this result but rather further shuts off individuals into the not-so-splendid isolation of pain and the inefficacy of self-absorbed misery doesn't invalidate the possibility for repair and rebuilding of self and world; it simply reveals how difficult it is to bring these things about. The line between hope and despair is vanishingly thin. Moral experience, especially the moral experience of suffering, holds the potential for remaking our lives and those of others.

I know Sally Williams somewhat better than the interview material may suggest. I have watched her operate in her world. I have spoken with her husband, her daughter, and several close friends. These others confirm the conclusions I have drawn. Jennifer went so far as to say that coming to terms with AIDS had made her mother a stronger, more sympathetic, and emotionally and aesthetically more cultivated person. A mutual friend drew out an even stronger lesson. "Sally was like a lot of us, pretty self-absorbed, quite selfish about her work. Ambition can be greedy and blind. Now she is a different person altogether. Maybe it's her success as an artist. Maybe it's AIDS. Whatever it is, she is a better friend, and it is simply wonderful to see how active she is for AIDS issues, for her art, and her friends. Maybe the best is how clear she thinks and speaks about what's going on with our lives and our world. She says what needs to be said."

But the most powerful testimony came from her husband, Daniel. When I asked for his reflection on his wife's situation, Daniel Williams dropped his head, walked a few paces away, and stepped back toward me, shaking his head and pursing his lips.

"I'm not sure what to say. I've loved her for a long time, even when we were apart. When she fell apart . . . wow, she fell apart! I don't know the half of it. Don't want to know. It was terrible, and not just for her, for all of us too. I was angry and frustrated and had no idea what to do. The kids, maybe save Jennifer, who always tried to pull Sally out of it, must have been where I was . . . lost.

"I had to cut her off, or she would have ruined me too. That all changed when she came out, came back. I still couldn't deal with it, so I kept my distance. But I heard, I watched . . . she came back great. She made it. Better than before. By then I wanted to see her again, but I didn't know how to do it. I was feeling guilty. I had dropped her completely. She needed me and . . . and I wasn't there. When she had all those successes, I felt . . . well, I felt I didn't do anything to help. I couldn't just call and say, 'Here I am again.' But when Jen told me about the AIDS, I ran, literally ran to Sally. I wanted to be needed; I wanted a second chance. I knew I could help. . . . When I got to her . . ." Daniel broke down. When he was able to pull himself together, he continued, "When I got to her, she was great . . . real. Everything came out. Everything got said. I'm so impressed by how she has handled this. Who she is. What she has become. Nothing hidden, left unsaid. It's all out in the open.

"I think you could say," her husband went on, "we expected the emotional maturity, the making over of pain into art. I don't mean it was destined, but that it was inside her character, ready to come out. But not the advocacy. She has become political, savvy in a political action way. Where did that come from? Never saw it in her before. She wasn't a joiner of groups, a leader of groups. Quite the opposite. Sally has always been restrained. That's her beauty. But now you also get the advocacy, and . . . lobbying. Yeah, real lobbying. That still amazes me. That was always my side of things. But not now. I'm in the background. Oh, I help raising funds, but she is out front. Sally calls politicians like she was doing it all her life. Yet some way the whole thing fits. She is a whole person. She hasn't lost the artistic side. Hell, no; it's even stronger. But she can do it all. Do more things. Look at how she looks. She looks so much younger. And healthy. . . . When you think, it's incredible. She has actually done better, much better with AIDS. I know it sounds crazy. But I'm not exaggerating. This wonderful woman has come completely alive. She's making the most of every day. This is her best hour, and it's not a frenzy or escape. She's become more fully herself. And she is doing things, useful things, beautiful things, strong things, good things. She's doing it all . . . and I'm, we're so very proud of her."

TWO YEARS AFTER I FINISHED recording this interview, Sally Williams suffered a stroke. The stroke left her left arm and leg weak, so she now drags her foot and can't use her left hand effectively. She is also noticeably slower in speaking. She expresses sadness and frustration, yet she keeps working, and with the help of Daniel and her friends the gallery remains open.

It was initially dispiriting to watch this once greatly vital woman slowed and diminished. Sally doesn't paint much now. She no longer can give speeches or work the telephone for her causes. Her energy is measured in small doses. Her vision is affected, and sometimes when she is speaking to you her eyes seem focused beyond you. She stumbles, has trouble getting up from a chair or placing herself on a couch. She needs assistance. Daniel and Jennifer are usually with her, helping her navigate.

And yet even this devastating neurological condition is not a final defeat. Her sensibility is alive to color and form. She often sings songs from her past. She is still tremendously interested in her friends and family members and wants to know what they are up to. She still has a presence in conversations. You can see that she is fighting her serious functional limitations to accomplish what she can. After speaking with her, despite her slowed speech and difficulty finding the right words, you come away struck that this remarkable woman is doing all she can to make her much smaller world lively and significant. She is not demoralized, not depressed.

Sally's sad story is not completely without a happy ending. Daniel, chin thrust forward and fighting back tears, concluded: "We have been through a lot. It isn't easy. We are doing all we can. It's what you have to go through in living. You do what you must do. Sally tries. She tries, and she's doing what she can. All she can. Being with her through this, I have been made better. So have the kids, so has Sally."

We are all at high risk for experiencing some kind of health catastrophe near the close of our lives, if not sooner. We all will be faced with catastrophic outcomes that we can neither reverse nor do much to ameliorate. These catastrophes we must endure, suffer through, live with. Stroke, heart failure, end-stage kidney or liver or respiratory disease, dementia, and the complications of chronic illnesses from diabetes to AIDS all define the final months or years of life. They constitute the terminal danger that defines the end of life, and with it the moral condition of human ends.

None of us, certainly not I, can be a neutral observer of how our friends, family members, and we ourselves come to the end. Neither of my professional backgrounds as anthropologist or psychiatrist prepares me with the technical terms and professional theories to deal with this core human condition. The messy mix of emotion, relations, and values that we all inevitably find ourselves in *is* the human condition. So I will call Sally's struggle authentic, brave, admirable, because those are the words in my everyday world that speak to her condition, our condition. That is how I see her as a moral exemplar of how I want to face health catastrophe in my own life.

7

Bill Burt / Simcha Adler

In the preceding chapters I have suggested that it is insufficient to express value positions without clarifying their emotional, social, and political context. So an acquaintance of mine—a good-natured physician from an old Yankee family in Boston—asserts in a dry, soft voice that fiscal responsibility is what matters most. He tells me it matters more than social justice, more than family love, more than the Episcopalian Church, of which his family has been members for generations. When I have questioned why this value is so central, this otherwise mild-mannered, cautious, usually tolerant, and otherwise amusing middle-aged man fulminates, stammers, and eventually, when he is thoroughly frustrated with me, shouts, "It just is, that's why!" What he doesn't say is what matters so much he can't say it without breaking down in tears. His father spent down the family fortune and died without leaving a life insurance policy, so his wife had great difficulty raising their three children and, as a result, my acquaintance could not attend the private school he had hoped to enter or enjoy the social life that his wealthy cousins experienced. He had always felt like "a poor relation," he once told me. His own life has been lived almost in exact counterpoint to what he calls his father's failure. He is extremely responsible, but especially so in matters of money. If you remove the expressed value—fiscal responsibility is what counts—from this disturbing circle of meaning, you neither understand the value nor the man who proclaims it. This is as true for me as for those whose stories I have narrated. Hence this chapter turns to autobiography in order to describe my own condition—subjectivity, local world, moral experience—and to suggest how it may influence the interpretations I am offering. I will begin by narrating an interlocking set of images, emotionally loaded memories that seem to me to authentically express who I am and what has been at stake for me.

It is late afternoon on a Friday in winter 1997, gray, wet, and cold. I'm in Washington, D.C., as part of a small international meeting on global health that includes both experts and representatives of several funding agencies. We are sharply debating the development of HIV/AIDS prevention trials in Africa. The issue at the moment is the absence of treatment for African AIDS patients. I have something to say on this point, but it is a distinctly minority position in this meeting. I want to say that for the most fundamental ethical reasons and because prevention is unlikely to be effective without it, treatment must be provided for these patients. This is a position that the representatives of the donor agencies were not then favoring. I am reluctant to express my position because I am not an AIDS expert; rather, I have come to the meeting as an expert in global mental health problems to seek funding for poor African, Asian, and Latin American sufferers of serious depression and psychosis, and for those who are addicted to substances or suicidal. Perhaps if I antagonize the donors now, I will later on lose their support for mental health care. I think of my East African colleagues who practice medicine with AIDS patients without treatments that are widely available in North America and Western Europe. Seen from the perspective of what goes on in their practice, it seems difficult to speak of the very real economic constraints (echoed by just about everyone in the room) without at the same time pressing home the ethical implication of the humanitarian tragedy of facing patients without effective drugs being available. It is ethically unacceptable not to make these drugs, at the time in wide use in rich countries, also available in Africa, I want to say. No one else says it. Indeed, the consensus in the room is troubling: only prevention, not treatment, is possible in Africa. And this is stated again and again as firmest conviction. The time is running down. I feel a palpable inner tension: should I speak out on the AIDS matter, possibly alienating the major players when I turn to my primary concern, or hold my fire and wait for a more favorable situation to bring up a decidedly less popular issue for which I'm the only spokesperson present?

I feel my predicament in my chest: a tightening and, noticeable to an asthmatic, early signs of labored breathing. At the time, the tension seems more in the realm of emotions and interpersonal relations than in that of morality. But why isn't it a matter of morals? After all, two serious things—each saturated with value—are at stake for me, pulling in different directions. The experience that tests my agency turns on a conflict between what is at stake for the group and what matters most to me.

In the end, I do speak up about the imperative of providing the latest treatment for AIDS patients in sub-Saharan Africa, no matter how difficult the problem of cost. It has the negative effect I feared. I am quickly criticized for being impractical and, worse yet, for distracting attention from the all-important prevention issues. And the experts and funders seem more resistant to entertain large-scale support for global mental health initiatives when my time comes to speak for that agenda. I have made a strategic error, as one of my friends in the room later whispers to me. But I felt unable to contain myself, as if a deep core of fire were exploding out of me. There is a paradox here. In the guise of talking about the ethics of AIDS treatment, it is the ethics (and emotions) of my own position in the meeting that matters more at the time. And it is the passion and commitment of the others present in the room that signals that an ethical dispute, not just a technical one, is occurring. Looking back after eight years, it is quite clear that a major transformation has taken place in popular and professional values concerning what to do about AIDS in Africa. (In fact, so far has the pendulum swung that some AIDS experts fear prevention is being downgraded as most experts and policy makers get on the treatment bandwagon.) Yet, as almost always happens in my reckoning, the ethics of actual experience goes unvoiced.

From an anthropological perspective, ethics as interpersonal experience is crucial because values are rooted in our social conditions. Standard medical ethics holds that cases can be parsed into questions of patient, family, and health care professional choice where rational decisions can be made once the relevant ethical principles have been identified and their implications for the case at hand discussed; moral experience more or less disappears under the heavy weight of ethical principles such as patient autonomy and confidentiality. Stories of real lives are trumped by philosophizing about justice, virtue, and ethical choice in the abstract. For example, in the case of end-of-life care, decisions are made about dying with dignity, limiting or withholding treatment or assisting suicide, and addressing religious questions of ultimate meaning by searching for the right combination of ethical principles despite the fact that so little is known about the person and his or her life situation that the case is usually experientially flat and thin, the real issue being the principle-based analysis. From a psychiatric point of view, the situation I just recounted is troubling because it is precisely those concrete details of a life and a world that need to be taken into account to understand who this person is, what she or he wants, and what is appropriate for doctors and nurses to do. These same emotional and moral details are as important for understanding what the moral issues in the Washington meeting were for me as are the concerns for justice and equity with which I premised my discomfort with what was then the consensus about AIDS in Africa. Those details lead from story to story, so that a life unfolds around the value questions, and this becomes the human context for understanding what really matters to people. These are stories that enable my own life to unfold around the value questions that I take to define who I am.

I REMEMBER BEING A BUSY INTERN on the internal medicine service at the Yale–New Haven Hospital. The year is 1967. The civil rights movement and the anti-Vietnam War campaign are intensifying. America is on the point of exploding into a cultural revolution. I'm working twenty-four out of each thirty-six hours. I'm exhausted and impatient to see my condition (and that of the country) change. A teenager with a rare and poorly understood liver disease dies in the hospital. I'm the intern responsible for this patient's care. While the boy's body is still in the hospital bed, a senior professor of world renown appears on the scene. Dr. A, as I shall call him, is locally infamous for his single-minded pursuit of knowledge and for his fierce personality, which often leads to his being brutally overbearing toward the medical residents and nurses (the hospital's "lowerarchy" as it is put among us). He bluntly orders me to immediately ask the family (whom he has never met before and who are now grieving in the waiting room) for permission for an autopsy. His objective is that the liver be removed expeditiously so that it can be studied microscopically and chemically. Feeling that it is unacceptably insensitive to ask them at this trying moment, I suggest we wait until the family has had a chance to see the body and at least begin to vent their feelings. Waving my objection aside with a smile and rolling eyes, Dr. A brutally informs the family that for the sake of science there needs to be an autopsy performed immediately, before their son's liver begins to rot. Anger and rage erupt. The parents and siblings say no, in unison, and proceed to lay into my senior teacher for his boorish manner. Silently agreeing, I watch with foreboding as he rushes back to me. Grabbing me by the lapels of my white coat, he pushes me around the corner of the ward and up against the wall. In a commanding voice, his hands shaking with anger, he orders me to take the three biopsy needles that nestle in his laboratory coat pocket. He will distract the family; I am to run into the hospital room, lock the door, and take multiple biopsies of the dead boy's liver. I demur. He snarls. I weakly suggest we ask the parents again for their permission. He explodes into a coarse diatribe laced equally with imprecations and with not-so-indirect threats to my career. We face each other with open dislike. I murmur no. "Kleinman," he seethes, "you just do it, goddamn you. Do you hear me? Who the hell do you think you are? This is crucial to research. We need to learn what is going on in his liver. You do it, now!" I grab the needles he holds out to me, and dash into the room. I pull back the sheet, looking at the body—white, cold, slightly stiffening—but avoiding the face. Then, blocking out of my mind all the contrary feelings, I quickly jab the biopsy needles into the liver, through the hairless skin, under the taut rib cage, which now becomes discolored at the three puncture points. I stuff the needles, with their liver cores, deep into my pockets and run from the room. I rush past the family, who are still passionately berating the professor. I am too anguished to look or speak to them, even though I know them far better than he does.

I never again spoke to this implacable expert. Even when he slapped me on the shoulder in passing at the next weekly clinicopathology conference and ostentatiously praised me for what I had done, I lowered my head and squirmed, humiliated by the coerced deed. Later I felt equally ashamed that I did not bring the issue up at the conference before my fellow residents and other professors. But it seemed completely outside the ethos of our training, and an irrelevance to the science talk of the meeting. Medical ethics talk, as surprising as it may sound, had no presence there or anywhere else in our daily clinical work in 1967. Ironically, the lived values of that world—the local moral milieu—excluded explicit concern with ethics.

This episode probably occupied altogether less than an hour of my professional life of thirty-six years, yet it moves inside me still, like a deep flow of hot lava. This episode bothers me most in that I did something that I knew at the time was unethical; that what I did was coerced out of me in a cultural ethos where this was normal experience; and that I was unable to express my revulsion or any criticism but had to "eat the bitterness," as Chinese put it. The emotional and moral responses can't be separated from each other. They were there in my sensibility, three decades later at the global health meeting, when the micropolitics of the interactions with powerful others added a third side to my experience.

I have had many occasions subsequently to recognize my ethical failure and to observe how it makes me more vigilant and quick to respond to what is at stake in my life and in the events around me. I recognize now that what is at stake for me is the anguished sense I have of my own constrained morality. I see how limited I am in living the kind of life I believe in because of what is outside in my world and by what is inside me. And the fact that I know this alarms me, because I can allow a partial truth to stand before and obscure the whole truth; because I can be complicit with unethical acts and fail to protest them; and because I can deny what matters most to me and thereby deny who I am. I feel a burning sensation in my face and a tightening in my chest even while I write these words because I am ashamed of these failures. Yet this troubling sensibility has also at times spurred me to do what I felt to be the right thing. Shame can be a decisive moral emotion.

I tell this story because so much depends on understanding moral issues in this way: as an inseparable connection of moral tensions, bodily emotional states, political contingencies, and the particular institutional or professional issue at hand in the dramas and mundaneness of genuine experience. Think of Charles Jamison's bodily reactions to his own self-perceived immorality and his criticism of American cultural values as another source of his crisis. Winthrop Cohen's depression also illustrates that crucial nexus with his remorse and regret, and insistence that the military and society more generally were as responsible for his atrocity as he was. Or consider Dr. Yan's moment of truth, when he turned away from vengeance after the great trauma of the Cultural Revolution in China, only to experience defeat once again by the changing political, institutional, and moral reality. I have witnessed many such occasions like the one recounted from my own life, when in the course of living we comply with or fail to resist pressure that we sense is wrong because the atmosphere of the setting we are in and the players surrounding us expect us to conform and because, truth told, we too want to get on with what is at hand. And I have observed the opposite as well, as in Dr. Yan's dramatic refusal to participate in vengeance, when the embodiment of earlier moral experience together with the politics of the moment erupt in an inexpedient voice that challenges taken-for-granted assumptions about what is acceptable action. I'm certain my response at the small global health gathering is one such example.

WHY HAVE I FELT CALLED to address this subject? That question strikes me as worth examining with respect to my own background in order to clarify what is at stake for me as the author of this work. I had always been absorbed by experience, the local, everyday variety. As a child in Brooklyn in the 1940s, I watched with wonder the comings and goings, acute tensions, and chronic intrigues of a complex multigenerational, well-to-do Jewish family. Against the sweeping background of vivid stories of the Great Depression and World War II, heroic and terrible, these domestic tragicomedies were of an entirely different order. They were small-scale and self-contained, as if reflecting another reality that, even if framed by great external events, was not by any means insignificant; my family drama possessed its own structure and charm and danger.

I became an intense listener. And I heard many stories, some true, some I recognized even then as not so true. To my naive mind, though, they were all of an order with the biblical tales we struggled to translate in late-afternoon Hebrew school classes and with the children's classic adventure books I escaped to on weekends, only the family sagas were more absorbing. They were closer and more complex moral lessons about real-life experience, where the interaction between individual propensities and what seemed at the time like familial destiny could be seen to work through acts of impetuosity, brute endurance, and a host of inveterate failings, from bitter resentment to blind, grasping self-aggrandizement, so as to shape character and careers. These pathways were somehow simultaneously novel and stereotyped. They could be discerned in the actual faces, body language, and fine peculiarities of relationships of these family members and friends who sat in front of me in the heavy Victorian parlor, lighted harsh white in winter and with a golden glow in summer, like the stage of a small but lively theater.

I was not a disinterested spectator, of course. Quite the opposite. There were multiple familial subplots unfolding along with one master drama, and either I was part of them or they held some significance for me. My small segment of the family—my maternal grandparents, mother, brother, stepfather, and one particularly close aunt, uncle, and two cousins—was in the middle of what felt viscerally like a terribly slow, only occasionally painful, but inexorable and dangerous slide. Financially, my grandfather had made several investment decisions in the late 1940s that would prove disastrous. At the very moment when the suburbs were being built, he chose to invest in real estate in the downtowns of several small cities in upstate New York and in New Jersey. It took about a decade for this enormous error to play out. The properties he had purchased lost most of their value as the inner-city settings they were in quite literally disintegrated. At the same time, a square block of prime Manhattan real estate that he had purchased as a kind of insurance policy was taken away from him by the city under the rule of eminent domain, supposedly in order to build a school (which never was built). As the family's financial condition changed, so did its relationships. My grandfather seemed to lose faith in his four daughters and sons-in-law as successors to his business interests, and more or less gave up in investing in the future of his other business ventures: a major soap company and a small mortgage business, in particular. Latent tensions exploded into open crisis. One aunt and uncle, who had almost as much wealth as my grandfather, broke away, together with their three children, from what had been a tight family circle. Another aunt died of posthepatitis cirrhosis, and her husband, who was having an adulterous affair with her best friend, and son went into a kind of exile.

My aunt Rose and uncle Paul and my mother and stepfather did not change their expectation of inheriting considerable wealth, but their relationships began to show the strain of their growing sense of panic that the small family world they had known and taken for granted for decades was changing ominously. I could myself see—and it was regularly pointed out to me by my grandparents, who performed like a Greek chorus—that these larger-than-life parents, aunt, and uncle, though robust and engaged in near-constant activities, were unable to prevent a gathering darkness and overall decline. As their inefficacy or wastefulness worked its way toward the denouement, I felt like the proverbial novice who possesses the dispiriting insight that there was a pressing need to do something, but it could not be matched by what the novice had to offer.

Not least of the forces indicating a strong tide within multiple stories was the fact that as a child I lived with two family names. At P.S. 161 on Crown Street, my primary school, I was Arthur Spier (pronounced Spear). At the Brooklyn Jewish Center, my Hebrew school, I was Arthur Kleinman. Spier was the name of my biological father, whom my mother had divorced when I was one year old. I never met him, which I have come to accept as part of who I am, after years of anger, regret, and mourning. Kleinman was the name of my stepfather, who adopted me when I was twelve. (Legal notification was buried in New York's *Irish Echo* newspaper—not a place my German Jewish father would be expected to notice it.) The 1940s were an age greatly different from the present one when it comes to divorce and adoption. These subjects were stigmatized to the point of being taboo. Nothing was explicitly explained to me, yet over time I came to understand that there was a secret, and that it held real significance for me. I became an undercover detective of clues, working out what my dual identity could signify. There was something there that mattered so greatly that it tremendously concentrated my interest in conversations and stories. That my biological father never surfaced in my life and that the story itself was never fully clarified became a wound that required healing; it was a hidden compass, secretly orienting my responses. It heightened my sensibility to danger and led to early recognition that memory and history were not the same thing and both could be treacherous. It educated me in the insistent sense that I needed to see things broadly, beyond my world of wrenching affect and fog-bound remembrances, so as not to miss anything hidden that was potentially important; while at the same time I was aware that that parochial world possessed one overwhelming yet mysterious absence of presence: my real father. My grandmother whispered to me that he was the king of Bensonhurst, a wealthy real estate developer, but she would say no more. My mother said nothing, but when I pressed her (which I hesitated to do until I was in my teens because she seemed so terribly vulnerable on this one subject), she also whispered but gave an entirely different story about a much older husband, an autocrat dominated by his mother, involved with a real estate scandal that was in the newspapers for weeks, a partner who was a well-known judge committing suicide, a criminal case taking shape, and her desperate need to get away. I didn't learn more until I was in my thirties, after my stepfather died, and I begged my mother to tell me everything. Her love for me and mine for her had been so central that I had forgone truth for our tie to each other. But I had as a result a powerful need for others to enter into my life as father figures, moral mentors. It also gave me "a hunger for people," what Franz Kafka said "a born doctor does."

In these human dramas or stories, it wasn't the play of words and the cadence of telling or the power of metaphor that held my attention so completely, but rather what they had to say about real life and how they lifted me into the flow of actual experience, tossed with events and alive with characters but with the tide moving powerfully in a set direction. After hearing these tales repeated I could close my eyes and step into them, because they were about my family and its circle, and in truth I was already on the inside, part of the lives and the world that were concentrated by serious happenings into revealing with astonishing clarity their transfiguring logic: a destiny of progressive decline in family fortune and the growing certainty that I would never know who my father was and what, if anything, I meant to him.

I WAS TWENTY-ONE. It was the summer before I entered Stanford Medical School, and I had just finished my undergraduate studies at Stanford, where I concentrated in history. My parents requested that I return for these three months to New York. I found a job with the New York sewer system, a kind of physical-labor "internship" usually taken at that time, like the roadside construction crew jobs of holding the stop/go sign, by high school and college students. I knew academic studies and weekend athletics. I had the romantic idea that I should also experience what it was like to work as a "common laborer." I did this, I now believe, largely to cross my parents and grandparents, who had what I regarded as a typically biased Jewish business-class view of manual workers as brutal, unthinking, and un-Jewish. A rebel since choosing to attend a distant West Coast university, I had incorporated a Marxist critique of capitalist society; I was ready to side with the working class. Besides, the job paid well enough that I could save money, so when I returned to medical school I would be able to live with friends in an apartment in Palo Alto, a chance to break free of dorms. After four years I had had enough of dorms. I had never done real physical labor for pay—working as a waiter and athletic counselor in summer camp hardly seemed to justify that muscular term. And I had never been anywhere near the inside of sewers.

The first day on the job the stench of the sewer paralyzed me: I couldn't orient myself in the dark, dirty subterranean world, and I was overpowered by the odor of feces, urine, and all the other "unclean" things that run into the sewer system. The slime and the pest-infested shadows, the foul air and the putrid odor made me retch, then search for the ladder to get out into fresh air. Only hours into the job I was ready to call it quits. I could not imagine how I could descend every workday for twelve weeks into the terrible stench and darkness.

Then, as I stood still at the bottom of the ladder in the midst of it all, fighting panic and a rising suspicion that I wasn't tough enough, one of the three co-workers on that initial foray, Bill Burt, a heavyset, white-haired Irishman with a cherubic face always set in an ironic smile accompanied by a constant patter of jokes, laughter, one-line quotations, and bits of song, grabbed me by the shoulder with his great ham of a hand, keeping me from bolting but also almost knocking me into the repulsive stream of sewage. "You'll be okay, kid. After a week you won't even smell it; a week after that you won't hesitate to eat a snack while poking around in all the shit. And after that you'll feel you're missing something when you're away from it."

Boisterous and piratical, like Stevenson's Long John Silver, Bill winked at me, ostentatiously pulled a Hershey bar out of his pocket, and broke it in half, offering me one part while he devoured the other. Then, as I gagged and waved away his offering and continued to gasp for breath, he initiated me in the local betting pool, the numbers game. Could I guess how many condoms would float by in the flowing muck in a fifteen-minute period? Each day all the workers waged a nickel, a dime, a quarter, or a few bucks to pick the right number, which was ascertained as an average across different districts. Enough could be made to pay for a dinner for two, he remarked, raising his bushy eyebrows approvingly. In spite of my unsettled state, I couldn't help but laugh and bet a nickel on a figure Bill told me was so outrageously high that it had never, in his thirty years in the sewers, been observed. That same day, he duly sent me to the utility truck to fetch a left-handed wrench. I could hear Bill and the others roar in laughter as I earnestly went about the impossible quest of determining which wrench was left-handed. When I finally gave up and returned to inquire innocently what were the distinguishing features of such a wrench, the laughter, if anything, was greater still. When Bill told me the punch line—there ain't any such thing—his voice was warm and sympathetic. "Never mind," he said, "a couple of weeks and you'll be a master of sewer work."

That day—the longest one in my life save for the first day of my hospital internship—our supervisor (Bill called him the Appalling Boss), Harold Wilson, took me aside and in his pinched, high-pitched Yankee voice warned me, in so false a fashion that even I (the tyro) could detect the cloying dishonesty, that I should be very careful working with Bill. He'd teach me bad habits, Harold complained. He'd turn everything into a joke, slack off and cover up for it more shrewdly than Brer Rabbit, cut corners, and show me what it was like to just put in time. His finger against his nose, Harold whispered that he would take it upon himself to educate me right. The first lesson was to observe what he would himself do that very day after work. "You warm up a little soup. You put it in any old jar, and you bring it to elderly widows in the neighborhood. I've got two on my block. You do that, son, and you will not only be a good person, but one day one of those old gals will leave you some money after they pass on. That's building for the future. That's how you can make some money in life!" he intoned with such seriousness that he looked like he could strangle his neighbors if they failed to comply. That was Harold, Bill would say, shaking his head: stingy, calculating, duplicitous, self-righteous, and dangerously earnest.

Much of the workday Bill organized so we could avoid Harold and thwart his hectoring, self-serving directions. Harold would send us on a mission to fix a broken meter, locate a sewer break, or deal with a backed-up pipe with an overly serious admonition to do it slowly, by the book, and in a way that would avoid problems. Avoiding problems, he told us, was the ticket to success. Don't make waves. If it was beyond our skills, we should call for help and then it wouldn't be our responsibility. Punt it to some other group if we could. Let them fuck up, not us. We should report problems, not failures—it was better never to have tried to fix anything than to get caught screwing up. "I don't want problems on my watch," he lectured us.

We spent hours in the utility vehicle with the two-way radio turned off so that Harold couldn't reach us, resting between jobs that we completed with lightning speed but effectively. (Bill would later report to Harold that we were in the sewer system, so we turned the radio off to save its battery.) When emergencies were announced—when our radio was on, that is—we were usually the first to respond, driving Harold into a fury ("Goddamn it, let others do it. Suppose something goes wrong. We get blamed," he would fulminate).

Bill guided me through the difficulties and occasional dangers of the work. We never did anything by the book, mostly to save time and do it right, as he would say, but also to annoy

Harold, who was a stickler for working through the details so that we could slow things down and avoid new jobs. We did things Burt's way, as it was known among our co-workers, meaning doing routine maintenance quickly but to a high standard so that we could respond rapidly to crises, making a dull routine more exciting and "doing some good in the world." It also meant more time to schmooze and less time exposed to noxious fumes and raw sewage. Bill twice saved me when I slipped on the slick catwalks bordering the river of waste that had swollen into torrents when the runoff from summer squalls found its way into the sewer system. One of those times I was hanging on to a railing with one hand, my other holding a heavy hammer, while my feet flailed in the space above the flow. Bill pulled me to my feet, admonishing me, "Don't do that—it'll mess your hair." He taught me how to open and close huge valves that regularly got stuck, how to accurately reset ancient meters that were nearly impossible to read even with the flashlight shining directly on them; how to unclog a blocked pipe—a messy business; how to repair an electrical wire; how to quickly evaluate what was wrong with one of the enormous pumps and consult with the on-call engineer to come up with a long-term fix instead of the proverbial chewing gum and duct tape; and how to think coolly under pressure, like the time we seemed trapped in a smallish space with foul air, unable to get the sewer cover opened, and three of our team panicked and ran in the wrong direction. Bill became deadly serious that time. "Don't ever do that, son, don't ever panic. Stay cool and think hard," he warned me as he worked out a way to signal our distress and position so others could get us out.

He was proud of my education. Some days he brought in newspaper articles he clipped, usually ones about misman-agement, waste, or corruption in the city. When I got into a shouting match with Harold about discrimination toward blacks (Harold had told me they would never work on his team while he was boss and that I was "one of those nigger-loving Jews"), Bill used his humor to bring it to an end before Harold actually fired me, which he had threatened to do. When I got into a fistfight after being called a "soft Jew boy" by one of the rougher workers, Bill grabbed the man's arm as he reached for a wrench. He then pushed me to the side and threatened my adversary with the same wrench. Later that day Bill pressured me to apologize to my enemy and buy him a carton of cigarettes "before he finds a way—and he will, believe me—to really hurt you." I watched in concern as Bill broke up a fight between four teenagers with chains and bats on one of the more violent streets in our area. Others were looking on, but only Bill stepped forward and with his quick patter and jokes and the lie that the police were already on their way got the combatants to disperse. Bill also responded to a dog attack and drove a snarling German shepherd away from an elderly man, to whom we ended up, against the regu-lations, giving a ride to his apartment house, for which Harold berated us daily for a week ("If you are going to be good Sa-maritans, do it on your time, in your car, and make sure he pays you for it!"). Bill shrugged off this pitiless remark and told me, "We're here to do good in this world. We're only little people, but when you can, you do what you can."

But most of the time, sitting in the truck or back at the base, Bill would take out his corncob pipe and tell me stories. I learned how he had come to resign himself to a job that others dismissed as beneath them, which in his joking manner Bill admitted was literally true. But humor and constant chatter couldn't disguise the disappointment and humiliation in his eyes when he talked about growing up dirt poor in Brooklyn's notorious Pig Town slum, dropping out of school in the eighth grade, learning about life by running errands for the Mafia on the waterfront, marrying a girl he didn't love after she became pregnant, carrying on in a dreadful family relationship decade after decade with two daughters who always sided with his sour wife and were as unfaithful as she had been, and coming to terms with work aspirations that had spiraled downward to "just marking time." Bill had two years to go until he could take early retirement on a small pension. It was crucial to him that he hang on so that he received that pension, which meant tolerating Harold and putting up with the petty corruption Harold and others organized as the everyday work routine. Workers bribed their way out of the worst jobs, pilfered supplies for their own purposes as long as it wasn't blatantly obvious, even spent work hours on second jobs (as long as Harold was paid off). Bill wouldn't or couldn't participate in this network of corruption, in part because after so many years he couldn't afford to get caught and lose his pension, and in part because it would degrade a reputation that had been built on opposing values. "Maybe, probably, I'm a jerk for not being on the take," he told me each time we witnessed a particularly egregious example, such as the time Harold traded new meters we had been sent from the supply depot for old ones and pocketed the difference. ("It doesn't matter, you know," the Appalling Boss intoned when we caught him. "Who can tell the difference anyway in this muck? And they all do it, all the way up the line, don't you forget it!") Bill once told me he was occasionally tempted to steal something for his boat, his one great pleasure in life and his hope for the future, but thought better of it when he realized how it would diminish his self-esteem, which was built on what our co-workers and even I thought of him.

The boat was everything to him. He had bought it from a salvage company, which had raised it from its watery grave, giving it a second life. *Lazarus* seemed just the right name. He had bought it for "peanuts" but had spent "real dollars, lots of 'em," fixing *Lazarus* up and keeping her afloat. We went fishing in Long Island Sound for bluefish with a couple of his buddies, and with such a decrepit wooden hull and ineffective rebuilt engine it was surprising the boat ran at all. But Bill beamed at the helm in the tiny cabin and promised me that someday he would get a more powerful bilge pump so we wouldn't have to bail the bilge water by hand. During the hours of trawling, Bill asked me to tell him about my life, and slowly, painfully, I told him about the secret history of my two names and absent father, about the humiliation that had caused, and about the academic successes that never seemed able to fulfill my vaulting ambitions, whose tyranny I could neither withstand nor understand. To say he became a father figure is to say what we both came to implicitly understand, though never could say openly, as the summer wound down and the time approached for my return to California.

My last day on the job, I took him to lunch and bought him a shrimp salad sandwich and vanilla milk shake, followed, over his protests, by blueberry pie. We lingered in the small snack shop with its sad oil painting of the Maine coast and its grimy counter and broken stools. We tried to joke about our time together, but it was a bust. ("You never would have made it in the sewers—no street smarts and too little ambition," he cracked. I retorted, "If I'm not there to do full-time bailing, the *Lazarus* will sink so fast you won't be able to tell your buddies those fish stories to keep 'em from wising up to how come there ain't no fish.") There were no words when I said goodbye at the end of the workday. Harold gave me a present, whose provenence, in spite of everything I had seen, still amazed me; it was one of our own logbooks, already partially used but with the incriminating pages torn out, now crudely wrapped in used Christmas paper. It was to take notes, he said, in my anatomy course. And the Appalling Boss also offered some parting advice: "If you can cheat, Arthur, it ain't a bad idea, but I hope you learned here how not to get caught." Then Bill simply stood up, his huge hand on my shoulder, and pleaded, "Go, go quickly, son, before you make an old pirate cry. Go, do good in this miserable world."

The story doesn't end here. I had a difficult first semester in medical school. I thought seriously about dropping out. Two of my friends who were finishing bachelor's degree programs asked me to join them on a trip to Hawaii. I was tempted but uncertain. I wrote Bill a long, convoluted, sentimentalizing letter about the importance of what I had learned from him. I told him my friends had in mind getting jobs as construction workers and living on the beach. I explained that med school was demanding too much time, and I felt cut off from "real life." Maybe I should just chuck it and become a worker and writer like John Steinbeck. What I had learned from my summer's job was that I could do things, practical things, I had neither known or valued before, and that I could be happy with very little so long as I could have friendships like the one we shared. I went on and on in this tendentious, maudlin vein, I now shudder to remember.

Two weeks later, I found a letter from Bill Burt in my campus mailbox. Bill had addressed it to A. Climen. The letter itself was painfully printed with a sloping line and sloppy end to each sentence and many spelling errors, words crossed out, and an almost complete absence of grammar. Bill had clearly been worked up by the fact that I was contemplating leaving med school. "Don't be stupid," he wrote, in essence. "Do you want to do donkey labor like me the rest of your life? Don't blow your chance. This may be the only good one you get. Do you want to live like I do: paycheck to paycheck, never able to afford things, caught up in the petty dishonesty of Harold and his ilk, unable to stand up and condemn the rottenness of work because you are too dependent on surviving to want to threaten the only adult job you have had and probably now the only one you could get? Do you want a dead marriage, awful, unfaithful kids, the bitter feeling that you deserved better? Don't mistake what you felt over three months for how you would feel after thirty years. Don't be a jerk and mess up. If you drop out of school, you can forget about sympathy from me. I will consider that you learned nothing. Poor working stiffs like me don't have no power. We are little people. No one need take account of us, but lots of bad folks prey on us. We get eaten up by big people. And worse still, we do it to ourselves because of resentment. Kid, if you give up on becoming a doctor, I'll come there and break your legs! You don't need to write back until you have an M.D. after your name." That is more or less the way I remember it—the words of a mentor admonishing me to recognize two different worlds and to enact the one I had prepared myself for.

BILL'S LETTER FIGURED IMPORTANTLY in another episode with a new mentor, a new presence, the following summer. Having somehow survived the first year of med school, and buoyed by Bill Burt's letter, I had borrowed money from my parents and grandparents and headed off to Europe to find the aesthetic and intellectual inspiration that had eluded me during the academic year. It was my first trip to Europe. I spent much of the summer in German university towns, where I could get by with my two years of college German and my small budget. I had a rich set of experiences, primarily with German students. I was relaxed, happy, and feeling better about the choice of medicine as a career. Israel wasn't even in my mind as a place to visit.

I have already described in *The Illness Narratives* how, near the end of summer, I crossed over the Rhine into France and entered a small town near Colmar. I checked into a tiny hotel and went for a stroll along the banks of a weed-filled canal. A squall blew in from the east, and as the rain rushed down I dashed for a distant copse of tall trees. I got to the trees with so much momentum that it was only at the last instance that I realized I was about to crash into the gate of a cemetery. The gate, with a Star of David at the top, flew open as my body struck its iron bars, and then the gate rebounded toward a stone monument with the names of the members of the Ruben family chiseled into the stone. You could make out from the dates of birth who were the grandparents and who the small grandchildren. They had all died on the same day in the early 1940s. That seemed odd. Then I spied more memorial stones, more graves, more of the same date of death. It must have been a natural catastrophe, I reflected, perplexed, as I stood in the open with rain pouring over my unprotected head. The rain stopped and I walked slowly back into town. But something dark and foreboding moved in me, rising and straining in my thoughts. I entered the hotel to find a different woman at the reception desk. I had no French at that time; so in a strong German voice I asked the receptionist what had happened to the Ruben family and all the other families in the Jewish cemetery. Why had they all died the same day? Looking back, it was an extraordinary scene. For the French receptionist, who had never seen me before, here was a young German student (seemingly even down to the blond hair and blue eyes) asking in blunt, unqualified words about the German invasion of Alsace and the Holocaust (the word had not come into vogue then) as if he had never heard of the Second World War. Not surprisingly, she exploded in an angry voice, reminding me that it was after all my people, Germans, who had invaded and occupied France and made war on the Jews.

I stood and stared at her. I apologized for angering her, told her I was the American who had checked in earlier, not a German, and quickly walked outside. I walked up and down the streets in agitation. The happy bubble of my summer burst into a chaos of dark feelings. I had again learned a fundamental truth about deep currents of history and memory underneath surface realities. I was shaken by my willful disregard of the war, the genocide of my people, the collective avoidance (which was widespread then and in which I so readily participated) of what had happened less than two decades before. And yet the way I absorbed this terrible truth was as if I were a German. The French receptionist had dealt with me as if I were one of the perpetrators. I experienced the two meanings—victim and perpetrator—simultaneously.

The shock carried over into the next day, and so I decided to explore the world about which I had been blind. I flew to Tel Aviv. The sense of interfused personal and collective crisis only deepened when in Haifa I contracted pneumonia. Put on antibiotics and referred to a youth hostel in the desert to recuperate, I spent most of a week coughing my way around the Negev. Finally I got on the bus to Jerusalem for a final few days before flying back to New York. On the bus, I took out Bill Burt's now dog-eared letter and read it over several times. Each time I felt thankful for the gift of his semiliterate prose.

"Important?" The tall, wiry, deeply tanned Israeli in the seat next to me smiled into my uncertain stare. "You've been reading that letter over and over again. It must be important," he repeated affably.

I looked at him. He wore tan shorts, hiking boots, a worn short-sleeved shirt, and the kind of white cap I had seen members of kibbutzim wear when they worked in the fields. His brown hair was cut short, and he wore a pair of wire-rimmed sunglasses, which he removed as he introduced himself. Simcha Adler was in his late thirties. He spoke American English, having taken a master's degree in agronomy at Michigan State University. He was now the leader of a new kibbutz in the desert made up of English-speaking young men and women who had recently made *aliya* (immigrated) to Israel from the United States, United Kingdom, Canada, and Australia.

"Want to visit us?" he asked, looking intensely into my eyes.

"Wish I could," I responded equally warmly, "but I've run out of time for summer travel. I need to get back home to start my second year in medical school."

"You really should visit," Simcha gently admonished me. "I'm not just inviting you. You were meant to be with us. I mean, even though I don't know you, I have this strong feeling that you should become a member of our group."

"How can you say that?" I answered, smiling. "You don't know me. What are you, some kind of recruiter?"

"You could say that," he laughed. "Yes, definitely, that's what I am, a recruiter; in fact, your recruiter."

"Are you putting me on?" I said with exaggerated seriousness.

"I've never been more serious," he replied the same way.

We both laughed and shook hands.

Simcha asked me about myself. I was bursting with self-reflections and emotional turmoil. I had had no one to share the tormenting jumble of feelings and ideas with, even as they deepened and became more acute over the previous week of desert solitude. Simcha was so encouraging, so enabling, such an intensely empathic listener that it all came out in one powerful torrent of words, images, sensibilities, stories stitched together by the golden thread of a young man's self-fashioning. My quest for finding personal meaning was hopelessly entangled with collective questions of class, ethnic, religious, aesthetic, and national identity. Through it all, Simcha looked directly into my eyes, smiling softly, not making any movement, and yet somehow he suggested that he understood. We were almost in Jerusalem when I slowed down and then stopped, drained by the passionate prodigality of words and feelings. Simcha said nothing. We sat in silence as the afternoon sun turned the stone of walls and buildings into golden hues whose intensity gave the sense that trumpets were sounding. Then the enchantment burst as the bus turned into the bustling, grimy city streets.

We walked from the bus stop toward the walled city. In 1962 this was the line of demarcation between Israeli and Jordanian troops who had faced off in armed confrontation, with most of the ancient city in Arab hands, since the 1948 war of independence. Simcha told me the history of how the Jewish paramilitary force had lost the Temple Mount. He gave me a sketch of where things now stood militarily. We retraced our steps and found a tiny café. Simcha ordered roll-up sandwiches of lamb, tomatoes, and onions together with cups of steaming tea.

"You want to know my story?" he asked so softly I could barely hear, his handsome head tipped backward. "I am a survivor," he almost whispered. "I was born in Russia, like your mother's grandparents. My family—all of them—were killed. I am the only one who got out. I came here as a kid. I'm now almost forty years old. So many things happened. I fought in the war of independence. Went to university, studied in the States, returned. I wanted to be a farmer. It was the return-to-the-soil movement and also a love of the out-of-doors. An agronomist, I had plenty of occasion to visit different sites. I found a place in the desert. It's very beautiful. Six years ago I brought together a group of young men and women who wanted to build, not just a place but themselves. We have a very special group. We share, we work, we sing and dance, and we get ready to fight. Because we are in a state of war. And small fights are happening all the time. We are border guards, and some of us are in an elite paratrooper unit. And me, well, like I said, I'm the recruiter. I travel around and find people, our kind of people. That's why I sat next to you on the bus. You looked . . . well, like one of us."

Simcha smiled at me, but his eyes had lost their intensity. He seemed sad, wistful. "We will be attacked. There will be war again. Jews will come from all over the world to fight alongside us. It is your heritage to be here with us. To live and maybe to die with us. To help build this land. To defend it. To stand up and defend the remnant, the survivors. I won't say it is your responsibility, because it is something holier that that. I am the messenger, but the call I bring comes from our people, living and dead. I call you on their behalf, on your behalf.

"Listen to me, listen carefully, Asher Michail," Simcha continued, using my Hebrew name. "What you hear is all that matters now. Your life, your striving can only be realized to the extent you find yourself as one of us. We need you and you too need us. So, can I recruit you?" This time the words were said gravely.

I really didn't need to think about it, and I surprised myself with the suddenness and finality of my words. "I can't join you. You mistake me, though I am not put out by the mistake. Don't misinterpret me. I'm American—a Jewish American, sure, but an American. I believe in the diaspora, not the homeland. I can't stomach exclusivity. That would exclude Bill Burt and most of the other people, the other non-Jews, who have been significant in my life. If Israel's very survival were threatened, I might very well come back as a comrade in arms. But I couldn't stay here with you. I'm not from here. What's clear now to me is I don't belong. I'm diasporic. I'm more sympathetic to the *conversos* than to the true believers. I hear you about the remnant. I feel the obligation. I'm complicit in the willful ignorance and denial. I will not fail to remember again. I am not the same person I was. I hear the screams of the victims.

"But when the French receptionist reacted to me as if I were a German, a perpetrator, I felt horror. Not all were monsters. Most must have been complicit. The horror was that I could empathize my way into being complicit, or at least making no waves of protest. Maybe I have too much imagination."

I had more to say, but Simcha cut me off.

"Okay, you're not one of us, but you yourself said when war comes you are one *with* us. Don't forget that! I'm not looking for bodies—I want the spirit. Do you hear me, Asher?"

"I hear you," I said very slowly, my eyes fixed uncertainly on Simcha, who was now once again smiling at me.

"You are something of a recruiter yourself," he laughed. "We will miss you. My instinct was right. Whoever you are, whatever you become, you have heard the call. You said no this time. I should be annoyed. But I'm not at all. I heard what you said. Who knows, maybe the diaspora too can haunt a person, forcing you to . . . well, let's just say, recruit. Go in peace, my brother."

I have never regretted this turn of events. As the Israeli-Palestinian conflict deepened, I could see the truly dangerous contribution of ethnic and religious nationalism to intractable political violence. The antiheroic stance of mutual self-critical reflection looked to be the only promising way forward. Heroism, in the classic mode, only perpetuated tragedy. There were too many recruiters on both sides. As W. H. R. Rivers, whom we will read about in the next chapter, liberated himself to understand, moral mentoring can intensify danger unless it enables individuals (and collectivities) to break out of local dialects of moral experience that underwrite violence by mobilizing inhuman responses to threats to what we mistakenly hold to be most at stake. Moral responsibility is not itself enough; it must be balanced with critical imagination. Over the years I've never felt I have had that balance, far from it, but I can now at least affirm the necessity of the unequal struggle to somehow find it.

Maybe it's not a surprise that my diasporic identification has weakened over the decades. I married outside the faith, and my wife and I raised our children in a broad coalition of values: Chinese, American Protestant, Jewish. I remain deeply suspicious of ethnic and religious exclusivity. Our friendship network is a global one. This is also true of the network of students I have mentored. Together with my family they represent the closest and most important circle of intimate others. Since many postdoctoral fellows, Ph.D. students, M.A. students, medical students, and undergraduates have worked with me over thirty years, I should know something about academic mentoring. What I have learned is that mentoring turns on dealing openly with the complexities of moral experience. Encouraging self-critical reflection, but not dominating it, matters. So does the explicit recognition that we are here to do good in a practical way in the world as part of our moral self-fashioning. To accomplish that, we need to risk openness to being changed by others. Being serious about research and teaching means offering evidence that one possesses an intellectual project that really matters to oneself and to others. A mentor draws a young scholar or clinician toward the subject in a kind of apprenticeship, the final stage of which requires that the apprentice move beyond the mentor into an intellectual, emotional, and moral space of his or her own. This is not easy to achieve, and it is threatening to both, but it must happen.

At any rate, this is the context of emotion, meaning, and relationship that makes up my local world and my subjective self. Out of this nexus emerge the core themes of this book: the centrality of experience; the powerful influence of culture, politics, and economics that can make us complicit in emotional and moral untruth; the way danger and our responses to it make and unmake existential realities; the call of the world for responsibility and imagination and practical action on behalf of others in need; and the aspiring defeats and despairing victories—the quality of antiheroic everydayness—that make life unmasterable yet open to hope, unexpected transformation, beauty, and critical ethical reflection.

The balance between the elegiac and the promising keeps changing. Four shining grandchildren and an enabling family have carried me through rough times, on one side; on the other are the bravery and sheer struggle that Joan, my wife of forty years and research collaborator, has demonstrated day by day as she lives with a fierce and unrelenting neurodegenerative disorder that has ruined her vision, compromised her memory, stolen her independence, and shaken our bonds. No time is easy; no life is as simple a progression as an academic vita outlines. The only certainty is the uncertain course of aging and health and the inevitability of catastrophe. I could not have written this book in an earlier time, and had I tried to do so, the balance would have been far different, as would the understanding of danger. The existential is always our mode of being human, but what is foundational to living differs developmentally as it does situationally. We go on, and on, and on, arriving and departing from new stations, and neither the journey nor we ourselves are quite the same. Each age and station develops a different answer to the questions of who we are and where we are headed.

8

W. H. R. Rivers

I now turn to a historical case: W. H. R. Rivers, an anthropologist and psychiatrist in Cambridge, England, who was influential in the first two decades of the twentieth century. I do so for two reasons. First, Rivers's story is a strong illustration of this book's contention that moral experience is a key to understanding persons and their worlds. And second, Rivers himself formulated a critique and practice of reworking moral experience as the basis for changing people and their worlds through education, research, psychotherapy, and politics. And this became central to his own moral life. The story of W. H. R. Rivers summarizes the issues illustrated in the earlier chapters, but it also offers a larger social historical exploration of why the existential question of who we are in light of where our world is headed is so necessary. It

"At Cambridge you knock and enter. The room was beautiful, with its brown paneled walls, but nothing else was. It was in an awful muddle, with books and papers and odds and ends of anthropological trophies all over the place. . . . Then Rivers came out of his inner study, and somehow at once the room came alive, and the things in it were right after all. There he was, rather tall, trim, quick and light in his movements, in navy blue. You got a swift impression of straight, broad shoulders and a jutting chin, and at once of a tremendously alert mind. He shook hands, told me to sit down, sat down himself, said that no doubt I knew what I wanted and how to get it, took off his spectacles and swept his hand across his eyes with perhaps the most familiar of his gestures, and waited. . . . He was like a man suddenly come back from somewhere into a world which on the whole he did not like very much. Tea came up from the College Kitchen . . . somehow it came out that I had read a little anthropology, and even that I had heard of Cross-Cousin Marriage and Classificatory System. Rivers' stammer disappeared. The table was cleared of a book or two. For a brief time we pored over complicated diagrams of relationships. Only for a short time: the History was urgent, and out I came again, suddenly to realize that I had been treated, not as an undergraduate, but as an equal.

"That was Rivers' way, then and later. It was a great part of his power over men, especially young men."

This is the reminiscence of the English psychologist and founder of memory research, Frederic Bartlett, in Richard Slobodin's book on Rivers. Remembering Rivers as a presence at St. John's College, Cambridge, in 1909, Bartlett continued: "His power did not lie in what he said and wrote . . . but in himself."

"I had said good-bye to Rivers. Shutting the door of his room for the last time. I left behind someone who had helped and understood me more than anyone I had ever known," wrote Siegfried Sassoon, the celebrated antiwar poet who had been Rivers's patient at Craiglockhart Military Hospital in 1917. In *Sherston's Progress,* Sassoon went on to describe a visit Rivers made to him after Sassoon had returned to the trench warfare in France, been wounded, and was evacuated to a London hospital.

"And then, unexpected and unannounced, Rivers came in and closed the door behind him. Quiet and alert, purposeful and unhesitating, he seemed to empty the room of everything that had needed exorcising. . . . My futile demon fled me—for his presence was a refutation of wrong-headedness. I knew then that I had been very lonely while I was at the War; I knew that I had a lot to learn, and that he was the only man who could help me. . . . Without a word he sat down by the bed; and his smile was benediction enough for all I'd been through. 'Oh, Rivers, I've had such a funny time since I saw you last!' I exclaimed. And I understood that this was what I'd been waiting for."

Another sketch of Rivers comes from A. C. Haddon, who initiated and oversaw anthropological studies at Cambridge and was Rivers's colleague and friend for three decades. Haddon wrote in Rivers's obituary in 1922, "He regarded all human conditions as the appropriate study of psychology and ethnology [a nineteenth- and early-twentieth-century term for anthropology's comparative cross-cultural approach]. This is illustrated by his last phase when friends in London, knowing his interest in labour conditions, invited him to stand as

Labour Candidate for Parliament for the University of London. He agreed to do so as he felt that his special knowledge might be of use under the present critical conditions; it was not political influence that attracted him, but merely a desire to give his best to his fellow men; to quote his own words: 'To one whose life has been passed in scientific research and education the prospect of entering practical politics can be no light matter. But the times are so ominous, the outlook both for our own country and the world so bleak, that if others think I can be of service in political life I cannot refuse.'"

Near the end of her engrossing 1992 novel *Regeneration,* which features Rivers as its central character, Pat Barker, in an inspired creative act, "embellishes" an extraordinarily telling story that Rivers reports to his great friend and collaborator Henry Head as "the experience of having your life changed by a quite trivial incident." Barker has Rivers remember back to his days as an ethnographer of Melanesian society when he was traveling on the mission boat *Southern Cross.* A group of Melanesian islanders, recent converts, are on board, and so Rivers goes through his usual field method of gaining information about kinship and economic exchange. He asks the islanders what they would do with a guinea. "Would you share it, and if so who would you share it *with*? It gets their attention because to them it's a lot of money. . . . Anyway, at the end of this—we were all sitting cross-legged on the deck, miles from anywhere—they decided they'd turn the tables on me, and ask me the same questions." So they get Rivers to say what he would do with a guinea. Who would he share it with? He responded that because he was unmarried he would not share it with anybody. "They were *incredulous.* How could anybody live *like that*? And so it went on, question after question. And it was one of those situations, you know, where one person starts laughing and everybody joins in and in the end the laughter just feeds off itself. They were rolling round the decks by the time I'd finished. And suddenly I realized that *anything* I told them would have got the same response. I could've talked about sex, repression, guilt, fear—the whole sorry caboodle—and it would've got exactly the same response. They wouldn't've felt a twinge of disgust or disapproval or . . . sympathy or anything, because it would all have been *too bizarre*. And I suddenly saw that their reactions to my society were neither more nor less valid than mine to theirs. And do you know that was a moment of the most *amazing* freedom. I lay back and I closed my eyes and I felt as if a ton weight had been lifted."

"Sexual freedom?" asks Head.

"That too. But it was, it was more than that. It was . . . the *Great White God* de-throned, I suppose. Because we did, we quite unselfconsciously *assumed* we were the measure of all things. That was how we approached them. And suddenly I saw not only that we weren't the measure of all things, but that *there was no measure*."

W. H. R. Rivers (1864–1922), as these excerpts attest, was a most remarkable figure. Researcher, teacher, therapist, politician— he was a polymath, and a distinguished one, who at the time of his premature death at age fifty-eight was a fellow of St. John's College, Cambridge, a member of the Royal Society, winner of its highly prestigious Royal Medal, and, at one time or another, president of Britain's leading societies of psychology, anthropology, and folklore. Haddon hailed him in his day as "the best field ethnologist there ever has been. He was also in the first rank as a psychologist." Not least, for our purposes, he was greatly valued for his huge productivity as a scholar, his intellectual seriousness and breadth, and, perhaps most of all, for the sensitivity and generative quality in his friendships, teaching, and therapy. Rivers had a special influence on others, as the preceding examples attest, an influence that members of his circle identified as moral due to the enabling quality of his way of engaging others and the sense of responsibility that he brought to (and expected from) those relationships. Pat Barker's *Regeneration* rescued Rivers from relative obscurity, turning him into both witness and hero of Victorian and Edwardian times. Even though Rivers came from and participated in British imperial culture, he turned himself into a critic of nationalism, colonialism, and the class system, which brought such devastation in the Great War. And he attempted to reform his world. Beginning as a hesitant, self-effacing, even reclusive scholar, he remade himself as a public intellectual who took on the major social issues that challenged his times. His life story reaches across the eight decades to our era, signifying a different moral age and the transformation of both our outer and inner worlds. Yet I retell Rivers's story principally because he was an exemplar of remaking moral experience by living a moral life.

Born in 1864 into the slightly shabby gentility of the Victorian English upper middle class—his father was a rural parson in Surrey who had become known for his approach to the treatment of stammering, a trait his son suffered from throughout his life—Rivers was educated first in medicine, with advanced training in neurology and psychiatry. But he abandoned the clinical side of medicine early on for a research career in physiology—then the leading basic medical science, which was shaping the methods and subject matter of fields as seemingly different as psychology, zoology, and surgery.

Rivers was invited to Cambridge in the early 1890s to develop experimental psychology, and he maintained an active interest in psychology throughout his career. A. C. Haddon, another former physiologist, asked Rivers to join him and others on an expedition to the Torres Strait (north of Australia, near New Guinea) to study social, biological, and historical aspects of the local peoples who lived on the islands there and specifically to oversee the expedition's psychological testing of the native population. In less than a year of fieldwork, Rivers transformed himself into an anthropologist. He developed interests in kinship studies and other aspects of social organization. He introduced more systematic field research methods and went on to conduct intensive individual fieldwork, producing early ethnographies of Melanesian society and of the Todas, a hill tribe in south India. Indeed, he might be regarded as the first modern ethnographer. His research reports established a new standard for ethnographies and are occasionally still read in anthropology courses.

Whatever Rivers's scholarship delved into, he worked at with enormous energy, fierce absorption, and huge productivity. Yet while carrying on a busy, full-time career as an anthropologist, Rivers also continued his physiological research, studying fatigue and, most famously, collaborating with Head on an experiment on peripheral nerves that became one of the sources of his reputation in medicine, because it set out a new theory of how nerves regrow after being severed.

In World War I, Rivers returned to clinical medicine as his voluntary contribution to the war effort. His extraordinary talent as a master psychotherapist emerged in the context of treating shell-shocked officers, who were being diagnosed with psychiatric categories such as anxiety neurosis, neurasthenia (a then popular medical term for fatigue and related psychosomatic symptoms), or to a lesser extent hysteria. His most notable patient was Sassoon, a decorated soldier who was placed into treatment in 1917 after sending an open, published letter to Parliament protesting the war. A poet, Sassoon had not sought out a medical remedy but rather saw his act as public protest. His friend and fellow literary figure Robert Graves, who suffered from war-related neurasthenia, arranged for Sassoon's hospitalization in place of a court-martial. Rivers, as we have seen, had a great effect on Sassoon, who idealized him as his "personal Savior." But the quasi-religious relationship also protected Sassoon from delving too deeply into the "tortured inward self" of inexpressible homosexual desire that Sassoon and his friend T. E. Lawrence ("Lawrence of Arabia") recognized they shared. Rivers actualized a kind of protective psychotherapy, a talk therapy that avoided exposing deep wounds and aimed instead to enable Sassoon and others to gently and slowly rebuild shattered emotions and heal broken self-images. As much for himself as for Sassoon, who exerted an equally powerful effect on Rivers, Rivers created a self-exploration that placed the treacherous waters of sexuality off-limits.

As a military officer, Captain Rivers was obliged to either certify his patients as disabled and unfit for service or return them to the carnage of trench warfare in France. It was "the age of massacre," as Eric Hobsbawm calls it in *The Age of Extremes*: "One quarter of the Oxford and Cambridge students under the age of 25 who served in the British Army in 1914 were killed." Trench warfare along the Western front involved millions of men who "faced each other across the sandbagged parapets of the trenches under which they lived like, and with, rats and lice. . . . Days, even weeks of unceasing artillery bombardment—what a German writer later called 'hurricanes of steel'—were to 'soften up' the enemy and drive him underground, until at the right moment waves of men climbed over the parapet, usually protected by coils and webs of barbed wire, into 'no-man's land,' a chaos of waterlogged shell-craters, ruined tree-stumps, mud and abandoned corpses, to advance into the machine-guns that mowed them down."

Not surprisingly, men broke down under the immense stress. The term *shell-shocked* was popularly applied; it conveyed the erroneous but culturally legitimizing idea that physical trauma, such as concussion, from bombardment with high-explosive munitions was responsible for the symptoms. Those symptoms seemed to fall into two different orders of things: paralysis, mutism, psychological deafness, and other motor and sensory disturbances, primarily among the working-class enlisted ranks, and tics, stuttering, agitation, panic, nightmares, sleep disturbance, amnesia, and other symptoms then believed to be more cognitively sophisticated and emotionally rich, principally in officers, most of whom at the beginning of the war came from the upper middle class and aristocracy.

Today, shell shock would, with other symptoms such as depression and flashbacks, be diagnosed as post-traumatic stress disorder, by which psychiatrists and psychologists would understand the condition to have a psychological origin with biological and social risk factors. But the very presence of certain symptoms has changed over the decades, so the concept of hysterical conversion has lost its cultural salience and almost disappeared, and certain diagnoses such as neurasthenia are no longer used.

It was not lost on patients or physicians in Rivers's day that the symptoms served the highly practical purpose of removing the soldier from the extreme danger of the war zone. The diagnoses were stigmatized, and sufferers were popularly regarded as either malingerers, cowards, or madmen. To Rivers's great credit, he argued strongly that these disorders were based not on physical head trauma but on psychological trauma and that this did not make them any less legitimate forms of pathology deserving humane care and technically competent treatment interventions. Rivers's distinguished scientific career brought greater acceptance of the neuroses of warfare, as he sometimes referred to them, but there was still considerable skepticism among military professionals, including medical officers. Ben Shephard, a British historian of military psychiatry who has written a definitive review of war neuroses, describes two warring schools of military physicians: the "hard" school played down psychological issues for fear it would lead to huge numbers of men seeking this means of escape, and the "soft" school, which included Rivers, sought to describe, legitimate, and heal the serious and widespread emotional trauma of warfare.

Rivers entered the Great War, as he himself noted, with conventional ideas of bravery, loyalty, and steadfastness serving nationalistic ambitions. But unlike the vast majority of his countrymen, Rivers's ethnographic experiences had made him critical of colonial and missionary policies, which he held responsible for depopulating whole societies, among other bad things. In Melanesia, he criticized missionaries and colonial government administrators for undermining natives' religious ceremonies and attacking their core values, thereby demoralizing local populations, whose faith in the future dwindled and with it their commitment to social and biological reproduction. He moved toward a relativist position in the early years of the twentieth century, when, as the quote from Barker's novel suggests, he turned away from invidious cross-cultural comparisons and argued for the crucial influence of local contexts on people's lifeways. He explicitly rejected the racialist science of his day. Rivers's views were not conventional, but on the other hand, he did not oppose the war, at least not until its immense human cost as well as his medical experience and relations with Sassoon and other patients changed his mind. By the end of the war, however, Rivers had convinced himself that his loyalties had been grievously misplaced. He recognized Sassoon's role in his own "regeneration."

Rivers returned to St. John's at the war's close to continue his anthropological studies. He would transform himself again, this time as a public intellectual, comfortable with a wide network of influential acquaintances, planning the future development of his several professional fields from positions of leadership, outspoken on current affairs, delving into working-class issues and socialist connections, and recognized by his friends as more confident, happier, and more complete in himself. Again, Rivers drew upon his reserves of energy to carry out a prodigious amount of academic work. He died in the midst of the political campaign, running as the Labour candidate for the University of London's seat in Parliament. One evening, while alone in his college rooms, he suffered the terrific abdominal pain of a strangulated bowel. The long loose loops of intestine kink, cutting off the blood supply to a section of bowel, which then dies, spewing its fecal contents into the abdominal cavity and spreading infection through the blood, resulting in sepsis, shock, and death. He was unable to summon help. By the morning it was too late to do anything medically.

WHEN I BEGAN STUDYING medicine and anthropology, I viewed Rivers as a failed predecessor who had worked separately in medicine and in anthropology without building a bridge (now called medical anthropology) between these different domains of knowledge and practice—domains that had grown so far apart by my own student days in medicine at Stanford in the early 1960s that I was told that they had nothing to do with each other.

The descriptions of Rivers at the outset of this chapter evoke the issues that frame this book: experience, its moral modes, and where their changing forms and meanings are taking us. It is W. H. R. Rivers as an exemplar of moral experience and its vicissitudes that will guide our further exploration of his life and work.

Rivers got at living a moral life via the relationship between psychological symptoms and human values. A point Rivers

repeatedly emphasized in his writings on psychopathology—
he had to repeat himself and do so loudly in an age when
Freudianism was becoming the fashion, among the elite at
least—is that sexuality is only one of the sources of inner conflict creating neurosis, and not necessarily the most fundamental one. A more fundamental source for Rivers—how
could he have avoided it during the Great War, when he had
his most sustained clinical encounters?—is the instinct of react-
ing to life-threatening danger with efforts at self-preservation.
The army officers Rivers treated were, he believed, experiencing neurotic symptoms because of conflicts between inner feelings, largely unconscious, of self-preservation and societal and
military values that required them to be brave and steadfast in
the trenches, where they could neither flee nor fight but had to
passively persevere under shelling that appeared to kill soldiers randomly and over which they could exert no control at
all—a terrifying reality. Seen this way, the conflicting moral
worlds of his officer patients—their homes, schools, and the
military combat conditions they endured—were the source of
their illnesses. Theirs were moral disorders.

What little Rivers had to say about his own interiority takes
psychodynamics in a different direction, from sexuality to
morality. Rivers tells about his relation to Sassoon in his analysis of his "Pacifist Dream" in his book *Conflict and Dream.*
Sassoon, here called B., had recommended Rivers read Bar-
busse's *Le Feu,* a critical work that promoted his thinking in
an antiwar direction.

"During the analysis [of B.] I remember quite clearly that
when I was reading the [*English*] *Review* I had thought of the
situation that would arise if my task of converting a patient

from his 'pacifist errors' to the conventional attitude should
have as its result my own conversion to his point of view. My
attitude throughout the war had been clearly in favor of fighting until Germany recognized defeat. . . . Though my manifest attitude was definitely in favor of war to the finish, I had
no doubt about the existence of a very keen desire that the
war should end as soon as possible for the egoistic motive
that I might get back to my proper studies, which had been
interrupted by the war. I have no doubt that this egoistic
motive was always active beneath the surface. I was aware
that if I had been acting solely on my own immediate interests I should have wished the war to come to an end at once,
regardless of future consequences. There was thus the grounds
for a definite conflict in my mind between a 'pacifist' tendency dictated by my own interests on the one hand, and, on
the other, opinions based partly on reasoned motives, partly
on conventional adherence to the views of the majority, in
favor of a fight to the finish. The article in the *English Review*
may be assumed to have reinforced the egoistic side of the
conflict by providing the rational support that, owing to the
supposed economic ruin of Germany, peace by negotiation
had become possible. The conversation with B. must also have
served to stimulate the conflict, though it is not easy to say
which side of the conflict would have been strengthened."

Rivers concluded, "So long as I was an officer of the
R.A.M.C. [Royal Army Medical Corps], and of this my uniform was the obvious symbol, my discussions with B. on his
attitudes towards the war were prejudiced by my sense that I
was not a free agent in discussing the matter, but that there
was the danger that my attitude might be influenced by my

official position. As a scientific student whose only object should be the attainment of what I supposed to be truth, it was definitely unpleasant to me to suspect that the opinions which I was uttering might be influenced by the needs of my position, and I was fully aware of an element of constraint in my relations with B. on this account. So long as I was in uniform I was not a free agent, and though no one can be a free agent during a war, it was a definite element in my situation at the time that my official position might be influencing the genuineness of the views I was expressing in my conversations with B."

Therapy, like fieldwork, involved entering the local world of the patient and getting him to return in memory to the horrors of that other, most dreadful world of experiencing once again the faces of battle. Rivers drew on moral experience to affect his patients. By making them face what was really at stake—their survival and also their fears of disgracing themselves in the ultimate test of manliness at the frontlines—Rivers moved them toward a liberating self-awareness, including recognition of the untenable position in which society had placed them. His ethnographically informed method enabled them to see what was at stake and why it was so conflicted, even if it did nothing to keep them out of harm's way. Rivers called his psychotherapeutic approach—appropriately enough, in the sense I have given it, though ironically from the perspective of depth psychology—autognosis (self-knowledge). As his own conflicted story indicates, Rivers was coming to the transformative recognition that self-knowledge must be about not only one's psychological state but also one's social and political position. Rivers came to see, long before Foucault

and postmodernism, that power and knowledge were inseparable. Seeing emotion in moral terms required a psychotherapy that emphasized the surface and protected the patient
from losing himself in depths of the self that obscured the
connections to the moral and political.

I believe this is the reason why so many of Rivers's friends
took his uncompromising commitment to the scientific
method, and above all his uncanny ability to identify what
was at stake and influence others to engage it through the
force of his own commitment to a certain kind of mutual self-
knowledge, as evidence that he was in touch with the roots
of their moral experience. In other words, Rivers's therapeutic powers and his interpersonal influence grew out of his
ethnographic practice in the field, in the ward, and perhaps
even in the senior common room, a practice that started as
hierarchical and one-sided (in his early days with the Torres
Strait expedition team) but ended up as a mutual exploration
of knowledge about the world, authenticity of the self, and
commitments to practical living.

Analyzing his own dreams, in *Conflict and Dream* Rivers
observed "the desire for change and novelty, which is one of
the strongest elements in my mental make-up." We see this
in his response to the call to Cambridge, the reinvention of
the erstwhile experimental psychologist as an anthropologist
during the Torres Strait expedition, and the leap back into
clinical medicine in the war with its subsequent journey from
conventional patriotism to incipient dissidence. Rivers had
lived through his own mutations and believed in their importance in his life and in the lives of others. But he understood as well that such change, if it was to have a transfiguring

potential, needed to grow out of people's knowledge of their worlds and how their selves operated (or were operated on) in those worlds. That knowledge was not just any knowledge, but knowledge about the particular tensions and conflicts in moral experience.

The relationship between the moral and the medical spheres of existence could not, Rivers believed, be lodged solely in the individuation of the person. That dominant framing in psychotherapy left out larger societal forces—politics, economics, social class, culture—that powerfully constrained the local worlds of patients and therapists. It was the relationship between the moral, the medical, *and* the political spheres of everyday life that explained the sources of pathology and enabled or blocked the possibilities for therapeutic transformation. But engaging this broader nexus of causality and change led to more than just increasing the potential for individual transformation. It made social change possible as a source of prevention, repair, and remaking of a local world. This was the possibility Rivers actualized in his final, and incomplete, reinvention as a political player. It is the abiding challenge to the fields of which he had become an esteemed ancestor, even if not directly influential: medical anthropology and social medicine. And as I have tried to demonstrate in my interpretation of the worlds of experience of the protagonists of the earlier chapters, this framework for relating subjectivity and social experience is still a crucial one for theory and practice.

THERE IS A POLITICS OF MORAL PRACTICE in psychotherapy. Any response to victims of political violence—say, in Iraq, Afghanistan, Colombia, or Congo—by diagnosing them as patients with post-traumatic stress disorder (PTSD) and treating them for the pathological effects of memory but failing to bring into the treatment program the politics of violence and trauma and the question of how to live a moral life under those dangerous conditions is an inadequate one. The act of reconstructing the trauma of political violence as only an individual problem of emotion and memory places its causes and consequences beyond the focus of intervention. Seen in this light, Rivers did not mistake what the issues were in his psychotherapy or his politics. Ultimately, one had to remake a world, and that required remaking the self as moral and political agent.

Rivers flourished in a prewar and wartime era that emphasized an explicitly moralizing cultural idiom, one shared by his friends, colleagues, and students, most of whom were in positions of power and authority. The cultural messages concerning how one should behave and the ways of socializing young people into adult roles turned on themes of courage, loyalty, endurance, steadfastness, manliness, doing the right and decent thing by others, shouldering responsibility, and so on. These moralistic terms not only characterized that age's culture but established the values to guide emotions, sense of self, and what I have called moral experience. This moralizing and moralistic world enabled Rivers to exert his strong personal influence over others. He became a master at expressing this language and using it to advance his career. And, as we have seen, he was extraordinarily successful in his time, and received high honors and academic position. But Rivers began to understand that his era's norms and normality were dangerous, and greatly so. Unlike many of his contemporaries, Rivers came to see how the very personhood of soldiers, workingmen, and their leaders embodied values and emotional reactions that fueled the fires of war and through the political manipulation of patriotism created an unprecedented catastrophe. He also came to realize that the destructiveness of British imperialism, racism, and class-based social life grew out of the same cultural ethos of dangerous moral commitments. Thus, he concluded, men (and it was a patriarchal and paternalistic world of men he had in mind) had to be remade to remove the incendiary moral bridge between power and destruction. Different models of how to live in the world were needed that challenged the established moral culture before it proved too late.

So Rivers began to reject the very cultural values that had made him influential. He sought to assist Sassoon and other officers to rebuild their lives in a new, more enabling direction not by telling them what they should do, in the authoritarian mode he now regarded as the cultural root of society's problems, but through a new form of ethnographic psychotherapy that encouraged them to come to terms with the cultural, political, and moral forces that had made them who they are and that had placed them in such a desperate situation.

Rivers is an epitome of what Tony Judt, the historian and social commentator on Europe, refers to as the burden of moral responsibility. Judt wrote about how that burden connected the lives and actions of committed French political intellectuals— Léon Blum, Albert Camus, and Raymond Aron—to their times. Rivers offers another example of how the burden of moral responsibility can be handled in such a way that changes in the person can have wider effects in the lives of others and on crucial issues in the world.

Flaubert's expression "No monsters and no heroes!" is used by the scholar of comparative literature Victor Brombert to distinguish a kind of negative hero or antihero, "a perturber and a disturber" of the way things are. Brombert writes in *In Praise of Antiheroes* that "the negative hero, more keenly perhaps than the traditional hero, challenges our assumptions, raising anew the question of how we see, or wish to see ourselves." Primo Levi, the Holocaust survivor and author, is one of Brombert's exemplars, principally because Levi challenged the sharp separation between good and evil, and in its place wrote about the gray zones of life where ordinary men and women end up doing terrible things. For Levi the gray zone was a local cultural world where the moral norms and normality of everyday living, not just pathology, created horror and desolation. I have used this idea of the antihero to describe several of the protagonists of earlier chapters.

W. H. R. Rivers could have been used by Brombert as yet another negative hero or antihero. Rivers died before his political career went anywhere. His works, while influential in his time, were not transformative for anthropology or medicine over the long run and have largely been forgotten. He perturbed and disturbed the moral ethos of his day not as a revolutionary but squarely from the center of the establishment. He liberated himself from the very cultural values that had made him and his career. In living a life, Rivers showed, we need first to be aware of the dangers that are part of normal, moral commitments. Then we need to craft a life that opens a wider space for others to build their own moral careers, where they have alternatives to established norms and ways of being normal. And that, in turn, makes it more feasible for us to bring emotions and values together in a more subjectively enabling way. The direction of transformation is from our investment in others in our world to what matters most to us in our inner self.

9

Epilogue

N arratives can haunt. What haunts our memories is more than images and words, but the actual world of experience that stands behind them. The self-harassed man I call Winthrop Cohen was haunted by what he did as a soldier in the Second World War. For over four decades he could not transform the undermining memory from a secret narrative of atrocity to a public confession of remorse and regret. And he haunted me with his terrifying testimony of murdering an unarmed Japanese military doctor who was caring for a wounded soldier. He punished himself thereafter with unwanted elaborations of the dreadful deed in dreams and fantasies. There were moments in our therapy where I was truly disturbed by the uncanny feeling that the ghost of the dead doctor was with us in my office, a silent witness, remembered as a face, arms rising, and a crumpled bullet-ridden body, as Winthrop Cohen took the scene apart and put it together again, and in so doing took himself apart and remembered who he was, refusing any mask, telling and retelling the murder as both originating event and timeless present, a deed that could not be gotten over or passed through. Winthrop Cohen relived his past each day with astonishment, grief, and horror.

Winthrop Cohen insisted that I must not explain away the haunting scene, mask who he was, or justify what he did. Instead, I had to step into it and relive it with him, and not as distancing pathology, but up close in the choke and sting of normal moral experience. It would take me decades to free myself from the self-protection of professional explanation to hear what he was saying. This is also what life is, he importuned. Don't say it is inexplicable but technically solvable. See it for what it is and feel ashamed for who we are.

Still, Winthrop Cohen's demand for absolute authenticity, his lifelong loyalty to the despairing deed, and his unwillingness to protect himself or me from its ethical haunting is what I mean by aspiration in defeat. Just as Idi and Bill Burt aspired in the midst of occupational defeats for a better level of human existence and Sally Williams turned her own experience of drug abuse and AIDS into advocacy and activism in order to do some good in the world, Winthrop's penance through depression was meant to do more than flagellate himself as punishment. He was acknowledging something inherent in human conditions and protesting. Winthrop meant for both of us—all of us, really—to feel remorse and regret to such a discomforting extent that we would have to change who we were and what we did or charged others to do in times of war.

Winthrop Cohen, like the Reverend Charles Jamison, insisted there is a divided world and a divided self. The world of actual moral experience (what we are capable of doing) and the world of idealized ethical reflection (what we are socialized to aspire to or to not do) are separated for him by an unbridgeable chasm between what can be said and what must not be spoken. In the former, the space of ethical deliberation, we address justice, for example, while operating in an unjust world, and in the latter, the space of everyday moral experience, we go about doing what we have to do to get on with the practical tasks of living, and in so doing end up practicing injustice. Danger, fear, and power characterize actual moral experience. They too infrequently are acknowledged and addressed as simply crucial in the world of ethics.

The self, for Winthrop Cohen, is similarly divided. In his dualistic model, a critical, reflective consciousness vies with a passionate practical agency. The reflective self offers reasoned justifications for our actions. Yet those actions—what we actually do in living—are as much based in passion and willfulness as in reasoned choice. The thoughtful justifications are often excuses, made up after the fact, for things that we do that explode from within like surges of uncontrollable anger. The passion-laden, practical self is caught up in what I have called our local moral worlds, what William James called genuine reality. The reflective self is caught up in ethical deliberation and aspiration.

For Winthrop Cohen the actual worlds of moral experience and the practical, practicing self are filled with pain, anger, uncertainty, and disappointment. Of course, he would readily admit, they are also places of exuberance, ambition, and struggle. The ethical world and the reflective self, for him, are comforting and comfortable islands of optimism, hope, and certainty. That's the way the world is, the way we are; look upon it and despair, admonishes Winthrop Cohen. And in his unappeasing criticism, we can almost hear the tone of Old Testament prophets railing against the too easy acceptance of the reality of evil and the hypocrisy of holding self-justifying ideals that we know are not intended to practically address that evil.

I find this bifurcated vision, which seemingly matches the idea of actual moral experience and imagined ethical aspiration that I have introduced in the case studies, deeply disturbing, as it is meant to be, yet also misguided. For there is space for critical self-examination, responsible action, and moral transformation in the divided world and in the divided self. Idi's story and the narratives of Dr. Yan, Sally Williams, and W. H. R. Rivers illustrate the bridging of real world, actual self, and ethical space. Ethical imagination and responsibility can, indeed must, be grounded in the turbulent waters of moral experience. Even in the most desolate and isolating moral landscape there is a place for criticism, protest, and practical efforts for change. And yet, in spite of its dualism, Winthrop Cohen's unsparing vision is an antidote to the easy lies of nationalistic sentimentality and commercial propaganda that would have us believe in a cultural scenario of an absolute divide between polar opposites: good guys and bad guys, heroes and monsters. The capacity to divide world and self may make life more bearable, because we can have our cake and eat it too: we can recognize the moral and political dangers in living and claim that we stand apart from them in a space of our own idealized intention. This way there is no requirement for moral responsibility or for ethical reflection to confront limits, failures, overreactions, and other practical dangers in ordinary moral experience. It misrecognizes what is most troubling in experience.

What really matters to us is simultaneously what is most optimistic and what is most ominous. Winthrop Cohen changed himself, and he changed me. His protest had the potential (albeit limited) to change others and even his world. That the world has not changed that much is illustrated by atrocities committed in the Abu Ghraib prison during the second Iraq war. That the world can still be changed is illustrated by the public uproar, political condemnation, and legal responses to that most recent abuse. Learning to value the defeated aspirations of antiheroes and to see their potential for remaking moral imagination and responsibility is one way that we can transform what is most dangerous in what matters most to us into something better for us and for our world.

I see Yan Zhongshu, at the very moment when revenge on his still dangerous nemesis was at hand, inexplicably turning away to create an entirely different and frankly better moral reality. What does that tell us about experience? There was and is no victory for Dr. Yan; in fact, his eventual departure from the hospital and exile from China amount to a species of defeat. Yet within that story of disappointment, betrayal, and loss, there is something else that cannot be defined only as defeat. There is self-critique, protest of the local moral world and its dangers, and the potential for transformation. Failure, seen this way, is not entirely negative; it even can be creative.

Of course Yan Zhongshu's presentation of self was meant to impress me, and it did. Speaking in the safer context of the United States to an American China scholar already identified as interested and supportive of the moral resistance of intellectuals to political violence, Yan knew what kind of spin to his story I would find laudable. Assuming the moral high ground is a conversational strategy that Chinese employ when building a network of connections, and Dr. Yan was drawing me into his network. I can't be sure there weren't aspects of his experience that reflected other values, ones he could or would not openly express. Yet he himself claimed to be both victim and collaborator. He talked of things he had to do to survive that he deeply regretted. He impressed on me that over the course of his life he came to the dismaying understanding that his family's history of collaboration with those in power, resistance against which had motivated him to stay and work in China, was not only the norm but quite possibly all that could be done in bad times. No hero, no victory, no self-serving myth here, in this dark vision of our lives. Change under these politically oppressive circumstances would be of necessity infrequent, limited, and not for the best.

In Reverend Jamison, the possibility for transformation shifts from the local world to the self, and in a peculiarly American way through the self to God. Here the body is the site of a decisive struggle in which emotion and spirituality transfigure shame into salvation, pain into "a good, a very good thing." Imre Kertész, the 2002 Nobel prize winner for literature, himself a Hungarian survivor of the Holocaust, writes in *Kaddish for an Unborn Child* that "on account of the pain I live some sort of truth." What truth that might be for Reverend Jamison surely has something to do with his desperate need for self-control, which in turn opens a strange possibility for religious conversion and hope.

Still, his victory over unacceptable sexual impulse is transitory, an alarming triumph that has to be won anew each day. There is another sense in which this embodied ritual of forgetting and sublimating unwanted sexual feelings into sufferable pain is a kind of despair in overcoming. Reverend Jamison once told me that what made it all powerfully convincing for him was that each time he was not sure that it would be effective, that transcendence would occur.

In several of his books, *Victory* and *Lord Jim,* for example, Joseph Conrad features a protagonist who when first faced with a life crisis requiring effective action in the world fails utterly to master the existential challenge. Later on, after living a life circumscribed by this core failure, the hero is presented with another crisis requiring a decisive deed, and, facing down the fear of repeated failure, he triumphs in such a way that both he and the world are changed. I once felt that this kind of heroic action could explain how certain individuals so successfully tackled serious illness experience that in place of expected disablement they seemed to have miraculously achieved what I then called a supernormality. I would now argue with that earlier conclusion; I am more suspicious of the orchestration of heroic images.

An antiheroic interpretation seems a better fit with Jamison's case. What for Reverend Jamison is "a good, a very good thing" is for the vast majority of chronic pain patients needless suffering. The omnipresent advertisements for medications tell us that we need not endure any discomfort whatsoever. With the sole exception of "no pain, no gain" in the discourse of sport, pain in our society is a thoroughly bad thing.

But this is not how it was perceived and responded to in earlier historical eras or in greatly different cross-cultural settings. The local worlds of Europe beginning in the first centuries of the Christian era witnessed a deep, massive cultural revaluation of pain and suffering, a culture in which these experiences were religiously valued and even individually sought after. Pain and suffering created a new and special channel of communication with the holy, a means of achieving salvation.

Reverend Jamison's understanding of his own predicament by itself is unable to prevent the fierce demands of intruding sexual feelings. And his understanding is much more psychologically elaborated than the prayerful reflections of early Christian saints on their own pain and suffering. Nonetheless, his insistence on the salvific quality of his pain would have received considerable cultural support in that earlier era. In this sense, Reverend Jamison is an anachronism whose moral experience is at odds with his age, calling into question what religion means as much as what pain means in America. Had Reverend Jamison experienced his pain as God's punishment, he would be just as anachronistic and just as at odds with our times. Pain in twenty-first-century America is supposed to be not sacred and salvific but secular and pharmaceutical.

Sally Williams's story turns on the transforming potential of serious illness. For many, such transformation does not lead to good ends. Exhausted and diminished, patients often succumb to fear, loneliness, and desperation. And yet for Sally Williams and not a few others I have known, chronic illness can inspire hope and creative acts of remaking one's self and one's network. A new Sally Williams emerged from awful experiences of AIDS and drug abuse, and so did alteration in family relations, friendships, work as an artist, and her relationship to the public world of crises and policies. Sally's movement from doing for self to doing for others does not result in a melodramatic movie ending of health and happiness. Something more authentic to our uncertain and unmasterable human condition and to the long littleness, as Frances Cornford put it, and anonymity of living in mass society emerges from her story. There is in Sally Williams a quiet and never fully achieved nobility of failure.

In her painting too, Sally faced up to the fear that artists and writers need to overcome: namely, that there is some authentic thing in them that must be aesthetically expressed but that they have not succeeded in realizing in their works. W. H. Auden expressed the cold terror of this feeling in his poem "Thanksgiving for a Habitat":

> God may reduce you
> on Judgment Day
> to tears of shame,
> reciting by heart
> the poems you would
> have written, had
> your life been good.

W. H. R. Rivers brings us back from aesthetic to moral danger. Rivers succeeds in his multisided career in a political and moral climate of colonialism, racism, and jingoistic nationalism. His impressive influence on students, colleagues, and patients, as we have seen, owed a great deal to the virtues of a moralistic and moralizing age, virtues that he himself embodied. Rivers's experience as ethnographer and military psychiatrist led him first to question this moral climate and later to criticize it as a destructive force that contributed to the deep cultural and psychological basis for the horrors of the Great War. His ethnographic method of intensive engagement with subjects' worlds, his psychotherapeutic strategy of helping his patients achieve a critical awareness so that they could revitalize their moral imagination and responsibility, and his political campaign of social reform aimed to undo the moral danger and to reconstruct moral experience in a more humanly promising direction.

I see Rivers struggling to de-moralize his times, to unmake what was seriously at stake in cultural norms and in inner emotional normality. Rivers understood that norms in the social world could come into the body. Cultural values could guide our gestures, our posture, and even our emotions and our sense of who we are in the direction of what the group regarded as good and desirable. Thereby, we become normal and moral human beings—normal and moral in the eyes of a particular group or society, that is. For Rivers, this normalizing or moralizing process could create truly dangerous patterns of personal actions, if the things that mattered most to the group and society were themselves dangerous. Hence British army officers in the trenches in France and Belgium experienced the normalization of trauma as courage (and the reciprocal pathologization of fear and loss as cowardice). They either perpetuated the futile slaughter or broke down. Either way, normalization could maim and kill. Norms and normality, Rivers concluded, had to be refashioned. The moral had to be remade. Psychotherapy and political action could re-moralize the world and the person by transforming what was most at stake to serve the interests of peace and well-being. Re-moralization could break the vicious cycle of escalating danger so as to prevent the misuses and abuses of moral experience. Rivers never got to put a political action program into play, and he didn't live long enough to see the long-term outcome of his psychotherapeutic approach, so my interpretation runs well beyond the findings. It is enough to say that for Rivers moral critique and imagination and responsibility were the grounds for social reform and remaking the self, and the one required the other.

This book is concerned with how the large scale disorganized and disorganizing historical forces of politics and political economy transform our moral life. That transformation results from the interaction between three very different kinds of things: cultural meanings, social experience, and subjectivity (inner emotions and sense of self), as shown in the figure on the following page.

Large scale changes in political economy and political power, as are taking place right now in our highly globalized world, change the cultural meanings we take for granted and the collective experience we are socialized into, and with them the self also changes, so that what we believe, how we act together, and who we are as individuals also becomes something new. And that change extends to how we regard ourselves and others. The result is that suffering, well-being, and the ethical practices that respond to human problems are constantly changing as local worlds change and as do we, the people in them, become something new and different. I drew

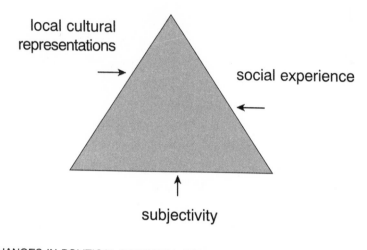

local cultural
representations

social experience

subjectivity

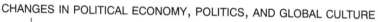

CHANGES IN POLITICAL ECONOMY, POLITICS, AND GLOBAL CULTURE

The remaking of moral life

upon this new framework to make sense of life in our times. If we are truly interested in national security, we ought to be quite concerned right now about what we and our world are becoming; about the quality of our (and others') moral experience and ethical vision.

And yet at the same moment one must be aware of other global transformations such as the enormous flows of information (including ideas and values) over the Internet and TV on an almost minute-by-minute basis that enable people to be more critical of human conditions, empower them to resist threatening changes, and encourage their imagination of new and different moral realities. This two-sided moral quality of our current era—the one ominous, the other hopeful— is crucial to understand where our world is taking us and where we may be taking our world.

A troubling yet sobering follow-up on Idi's quietly effective but low-visibility career arose several years after her untimely death. I was attending a conference where I met two people (a European anthropologist and an American expert in humanitarian assistance) who had each worked in one of the countries in which Idi had served. Neither could remember her, and the European anthropologist may not have met her. The American at first got her confused with another woman. When I corrected his mistaken impression, he shrugged and with a wistful air remarked that there were many, many people like Idi who deserved to be better known and whose contributions in the aggregate made a difference, but whose individuality, while seemingly vivid and indelible, was inevitably lost amid the blur of faces in the slew of humanitarian assistance programs that started, ended, and were reinvented over time. He went on, in a distancing philosophical mood, to opine that all individuals in the field had to ask themselves repeatedly whether it really mattered that they had come or if it would have made any difference if they had not. Lost in his own reverie now, he asked, did it even make a difference in their own lives that they had been in this place at this time with this project?

I remember walking away from that encounter shaken, feeling both disappointment and bitterness. I determined then to stop procrastinating and write about Idi. But in so doing, I have watched my own remembrances undergo a metamorphosis from a heroic genre to an antiheroic one. It was fitting, I came to see, given the view of moral experience that had increasingly come to inhabit my thoughts, for Idi to have been mistakenly identified, forgotten, or never met. After all, Idi was not the star of a movie, with all the celebratory, larger-than-life, dramatic qualities that role carries. As an ordinary person, she was, I had come to accept with regret, forgettable. She had achieved neither fame nor fortune; her circle of acquaintances, though lively and intense, remained small. After she departed Africa, a new generation of foreign experts had started new projects in shifting situations with different clients and partners. None of them had written or read the history of her work. And yet for me, perhaps because rather than in spite of these limitations, Idi will always represent what is genuine and best in us.

Saying as much makes me realize I am overstepping my warrant as witness and recorder of moral experience, as I did when I applauded a diminished Sally Williams's transformation through suffering from a "taker" into a "giver." I am moving from description to prescription, from the moral to the ethical, and that is probably unavoidable. What do these accounts tell us about how we should live?

First we need to get right what matters most to us. It doesn't hurt to try to peek beneath the layers of family, self, and setting and find the strands that connect to our present commitments. Hence, Idi was not unaware of the impetus for her parents' commitment to progressive politics, liberation theology, and works of reparation and restitution: her grandfather's collaboration with the Nazis and the selfish greed and hauteur of her mother's large haute bourgeois family. She also was not blind to the same influence on her career and life. Sally Williams realized her readiness not to be silent but to advocate for AIDS and drug abuse programs was intensified by her early experiences of a secret, unspeakable world of family violence, alcoholism, and depression. In Bill Burt and Simcha Adler, and in later mentors, I came to see the absence of presence of my own father, and the pressing need for father figures in my own self-building. And this led to a further recognition of why I so urgently needed to be a mentor and healer to others, and perhaps also to why I initially searched for moral heroes.

This same process of autognosis, to use Rivers's term for becoming acutely self-aware of the forces that are shaping us and the directions toward which they are moving us, enables us to see how the bundle of contradictions, incompatibilities, mindless routine, and the bewildering inexpediency of one damn thing following another and of countless, cross-cutting personal projects resisting realization of our plans prevents us from examining too hard and too critically the deep existential structure of our lives. It just may not be possible to act in the world and at the same time admit fully the dangers around us and the limits to coping, and to accept our end not just in suffering and death but in the smallness, ill-suitedness, and forgettable quality to our lives and work. That is what makes moral experience so difficult and disappointingly human.

Eventually, we need to ask the question few of us ever want to address directly: what *should* really matter? In this book I am making the case for facing up to our existential condition as what really matters. Underneath the huge varieties of cultural meanings, social experiences, and subjectivity, there is a shared condition of being human that centers on experiences of loss, threat, and uncertainty. That is ground zero in our moral lives. Yet my career as a psychiatrist and anthropologist convinces me that there can be no single thing that matters most for each of us or for all of us. The differences, as these chapters show, can be striking. But as troubling and uncertain as it is to come to terms with what matters in the actual conditions of our worlds and our lives, I have come to believe that this is the way to be authentic and useful in crafting a life.

In his short story "The Middle Years," Henry James puts words in the mouth of a dying writer who is being tended to by a young physician who himself harbors a secret desire to be a writer. The writer means to mentor the doctor (both as healer and artist) by conveying a single truth about life and career: " We work in the dark—we do what we can—we give what we have. Our doubt is our passion and passion is our task." We are passionately anxious about doubt, I take it, because it threatens to undermine self-control, undo competence, and, in the sense of this book, dislocate and distort those aspects of moral experience that are most enabling while giving expression to others that can be truly dangerous. Doubt in itself—a feeling of uncertainty and a need to call things into question—is also what we must be passionate about because we must interrogate our moral life. Passion is our task because competence and even engagement without passion would never lead to the kind of commitment Idi made, or to Dr. Yan's transfiguration of vengeance into healing, or to any expression of our deepest sense of who we are and what we are about that ran against the grain of convention and conformity. Passion is absolutely required in the unequal struggle to master human experience, or else we would succumb to comforting self-illusions and the merely mechanical requirements of social life and ultimately to demoralization. A passion for doubting is a requirement of a moral life because we need to bring an aspiration for ethics to bear on moral experience, and ethical enquiry and action are impelled when doubt is our passion and passion is our task. In yet another sense—namely, when passion means to afflict with suffering—Henry James's penetrating words resonate with our responsibility to take seriously the existential limits of our human condition. But it is just as important to understand that passion plays off joy, irony, and humor, which also are crucial qualities in getting through life.

How, then, to live? What to do? Those huge questions are foundational to ethics, religion, and political theory. They are not ones that I am prepared to answer with a specific prescription for living. I barely am able to muddle through; I have no such prescription. No one does, I contend. Still, what a lifetime of being with others in the messiness of moral experience has taught me is that simplistic distinctions between the objective and the subjective, the absolute and the relative, the right and the wrong, are no help and may even get us into deeper trouble. Nor is it at all sufficient to take up a position in which complexity, uncertainty, and undecidability negate the vexing questions themselves, covering over our own weaknesses and self-serving willingness to comply as long as we are comfortable and protected, as long as the future brings clean bathrooms and an air control system. That way leads to a hollowing out of passion and purpose, to cynicism and nihilism, and ultimately disables us and denies us the capability to change ourselves and our world.

Commitment to others, struggling to bring some good into our close-up worlds even while acknowledging that our coping skills are barely adequate, being passionate about projects that build the self and others, being serious about critical engagement steeped in self-reflection and aimed to rework or stop moral processes that intensify danger, mobilizing aspiration in defeat and finding the courage and endurance even when experiencing the hollowness of victories not to completely despair—those are the kinds of things that, no matter their trite and conventional ring, still feel authentic and useful. The authentic and useful, especially in a time when commercial propaganda and the politically meretricious are so ubiquitous, are still something, as are kindness and decency—insisting, as Emmanuel Lévinas did, that the ethical precedes the epistemological, that acknowledgment and affirmation of the other precedes inquiry and enables a readiness for unexpected transformations, which do occur and can be revitalizing if seized hold of and properly directed. We must see moral experience for what it is: all that we have and all that we will ever have that defines our humanity and makes us and our worlds real.

Pablo Picasso © ARS, NY. Head of a Medical Student, (Study for Les Demoiselles d'Avignon) 1907. Conger Goodyear Fund, Museum of Modern Art, USA. *Digital Image © The Museum of Modern Art / Licensed by SCALA / Art Resource, NY*

I have long found arresting a painting of Pablo Picasso's titled "The Head of a Medical Student". The painting is of a face in the form of an African mask with one eye open, and the other closed. Medical students learn to open one eye to the pain and suffering of patients and the world, but also to close the other eye—to protect their own vulnerability to pain and suffering, to protect their belief that they can do good and change the world for the better, to protect their own self-interests such as career building and economic gain. I would generalize the provocative poignancy of this picture to how we live our lives. One of our eyes is open to the dangers of the world and the uncertainty of our human condition; the other is closed, so that we do not see or feel these things, so that we can get on with our lives. But perhaps one eye is closed so that we can see, feel and do something of value. One eye, perhaps, sees the possibilities and hopefulness of who we are and where we are headed, while the other is shut tight with fear over the storms and precipices that lie ahead. Or, perhaps like all things human, it is about something else altogether, something else that mattered to Picasso, because when I look at others of his paintings that feature faces formed as African masks, one eye often seems closed—a perturbing matter of style or a disturbing matter of existential insight?

Bibliographic Note

To make this book accessible for the educated general reader, whose time for reading is limited and who almost surely doesn't want to get bogged down in excessive detail, I have written it without the scholarly scaffolding of footnotes and academic references to the research literature. But both because I am myself, as a researcher and teacher, somewhat uneasy about this absence and because there may be readers whose interests are piqued sufficiently to want to read further into this perspective on moral experience, I am setting out a short list of relevant works that form the research and theoretical basis for the positions I have advanced.

On the question of moral experience, the literature in philosophy, phenomenology, and social theory is large. I summarize key works—e.g., those by John Dewey, William James, Michael Oakshott, and many others—in the Tanner Lectures I delivered at Stanford University in 1998, where I also show how medical anthropology, social medicine, and cultural psychiatry offer research that underpins the theory I advance. See Arthur Kleinman, "Experience and Its Moral Modes: Culture, Human Conditions, and Disorder," in G. B. Peterson, ed., *The Tanner Lectures on Human Values* (Salt Lake City: University of Utah Press, 1999), 20:357–420. (This scholarly essay also can be downloaded from the Web at www.tannerlectures.utah.edu.) A shorter version with more of a global health policy thrust can be found in Arthur Kleinman, "Ethics and Experience: An Anthropological Approach to Health Equity," in Sudhir Anand,

Fabienne Peter, and Amartya Sen, eds., *Public Health, Ethics and Equity*, 269–82 (Oxford: Oxford University Press, 2004).

Contributions to the anthropological approach to moral experience, including works that deal with social aspects of moral life, are Talal Asad, *Genealogies of Religion: Discipline and Reasons of Power in Christianity and Islam* (Baltimore, MD: Johns Hopkins University Press, 1993); João Biehl, *Vita: Life in a Zone of Abandonment* (Berkeley: University of California Press, 2005); Pierre Bourdieu, *The Logic of Practice* (Stanford: Stanford University Press, 1990); Pierre Bourdieu, ed., *La Misère du Monde* (Paris: Editions du Seuil, 1993); Georges Canguilhem, *The Normal and the Pathological* (New York: Zone Books, 1991); Rebecca S. Chopp, *The Praxis of Suffering: An Interpretation of Liberation and Political Theologies* (Maryknoll, NY: Orbis Books, 1986); Lawrence Cohen, *No Aging in India* (Berkeley: University of California Press, 1992); Thomas Csordas, ed., *Embodiment and Experience: The Existential Ground of Culture and Self* (Cambridge: Cambridge University Press, 1994); Veena Das, "Moral Orientations to Suffering," in L. C. Chen, A. Kleinman, and N. Ware, eds., *Health and Social Change: An International Perspective* (Cambridge, MA: Harvard University Press, 1994); Veena Das et al., eds., *Remaking a World* (Berkeley: University of California Press, 2001); John Dewey, *Human Nature and Conduct* (New York: Modern Library, 1957 [1922]); Paul Farmer, *AIDS and Accusation: The Geography of Blame in Haiti* (Berkeley: University of California Press, 1992); Ludwig Fleck, *Genesis and Development of a Scientific Fact* (Chicago: University of Chicago Press, 1979); Michel Foucault, *The Birth of the Clinic* (New York: Vintage, 1973); Clifford Geertz, *Local Knowledge* (New York: Basic Books, 1987); Jonathan Glover, *Humanity: A Moral History of the Twentieth Century* (London: Jonathan Cape, 1999); Byron Good, *Medicine, Rationality and Experience* (Cambridge: Cambridge University Press, 1994); Mary Jo DelVecchio Good et al., eds., *Pain as Human Experience* (Berkeley: University of California Press, 1992); John Grey, *False Down: The Delusions of Global Capitalism* (London: Granta Books, 1998); Michael Jackson, ed., *Things as They Are: Introduction to Phenomenological Anthropology* (Bloomington: Indiana University Press, 1996); Martin Jay, *Songs of Experience: Modern American and European Variations on a Universal Theme* (Berkeley: University of California Press, 2005); James Kellenberger, *Relationship Morality* (University Park: Pennsylvania State University Press, 1995); Arthur Kleinman, *The Illness Narratives* (New York: Basic Books, 1988); Arthur Kleinman, *Rethinking Psychiatry* (New York: Free Press, 1988); Arthur Kleinman, Veena Das, and Margaret Lock, eds., *Social Suffering* (Berkeley: University of California Press, 1997); George Lakoff and Mark Johnson, *Philosophy in the Flesh: The Embodied Mind and its Challenge to Western Thought* (New York: Basic Books, 1999); Roger Lancaster, *Life Is Hard: Machismo, Danger and the Intimacy of Power in Nicaragua* (Berkeley: University of California Press, 1992); Margaret Lock, *Encounters with Aging* (Berkeley: University of California Press, 1993); Margaret Lock, *Twice Dead* (Berkeley: University of California Press, 2003); Michel Moody-Adams, *Fieldwork in Familiar Places* (Cambridge, MA: Harvard University Press, 1997); Tanya Luhrmann, *Of Two Minds: The Growing Disorder in American Psychiatry* (New York: Knopf, 2000); Adriana Petryna, *Life Exposed* (Princeton: Princeton University Press, 2002); Nancy Scheper-Hughes, *Death Without Weeping: The Violence of Everyday Life in Brazil* (Berkeley: University of California Press, 1992).

On anthropological approaches to global health, see Robert Desjarlais et al., *World Mental Health* (Oxford: Oxford University Press, 1995); Paul Farmer, *Pathologies of Power* (Berkeley: University of California Press, 2003); Paul Farmer, Margaret Connors, and Janie Simmons, eds., *Women, Poverty and AIDS: Sex, Drugs and Structural Violence* (Monroe, ME: Common Courage Press, 1996); Jim Yong Kim et al., eds., *Dying for Growth* (Monroe, ME: Common Courage Press, 2000).

Readers interested in getting further into moral experience in present-day Chinese society (as covered in Chapter 4) can consult, among many relevant works, Jasper Becker, *Hungry Ghosts: Mao's Secret Famine* (New York: Free Press, 1996); Jung Chang, *Wild Swans: Three Daughters of China* (New York: Simon and Schuster, 1991); Jung Chang and Jon Halliday, *Mao: The Unknown Story* (New York: Knopf, 2005); Xiaotong Fei, *From the Soil: The Foundations of Chinese Society* (Berkeley: University of California Press, 1992); Jicai Feng, *Ten Years of Madness: Oral Histories of China's Cultural Revolution* (San Francisco: China Books and Periodicals, 1996); Jun Jing, *The Temple of Memories: History, Power and Morality in a Chinese Village* (Stanford: Stanford University Press, 1996); Erik Mueggler, *The Age of Wild Ghosts: Memory, Violence and Place in Southwest China* (Berkeley: University of California Press, 2001); Elizabeth Perry and Mark Selden, eds., *Chinese Society*, 2nd ed. (New York: Routledge, 2003); Orville Schell, *Mandate of Heaven* (New York: Simon and Schuster, 1994); Anne F. Thurston, *Enemies of the People* (New York: Alfred Knopf, 1987); Yunxiang Yan, *The Flow of Gifts: Reciprocity and Social Networks in a Chinese Village* (Stanford: Stanford University Press, 1996); Yunxiang Yan, *Private Life under Socialism: Love, Intimacy, and Family Change in a Chinese Village, 1949–1999* (Stanford: Stanford University Press, 2003).

For those whose interest in W. H. R. Rivers has been awakened, there is a small but interesting literature (both scholarly and fictional) about him and a much larger body of works about the tumultuous period in which he lived, including works on psychiatric syndromes associated with the Great War: Peter Barham, *Forgotten Lunatics of the Great War* (New Haven: Yale University Press, 2004); Pat Barker, *Regeneration* (New York: Dutton,

1992); Pat Barker, *The Eye in the Door* (New York: Dutton, 1994); Pat Barker, *The Ghost Road* (New York: Dutton, 1995); Joanna Bourke, *An Intimate History of Killing: Face to Face Killing in 20th Century Warfare* (New York: Basic Books, 1999); Henry Head, "William Halse Rivers Rivers, 1864–1922," *Proceedings of the Royal Society of London*, series B, 95 (1923): xliii–xlvii; A. C. Haddon, F. C. Bartlett, and Ethel S. Fegan, "Obituary. Williams Halse Rivers Rivers," *Man* 22 (1922): 97–104; Anita Herle and Sandra Rouse, eds., *Cambridge and the Torres Strait: Centenary Essays on the 1898 Anthropological Expedition* (Cambridge: Cambridge University Press, 1998); Eric Hobsbawm, *The Age of Extremes: A History of the World, 1914–1991* (New York: Pantheon, 1994); Ian Langham, *The Building of British Social Anthropology: W. H. R. Rivers and His Cambridge Disciples in the Development of Kinship Studies, 1898–1931* (Dordrecht, Holland: D. Reidel, 1981); Eric Leed, *No Man's Land: Combat and Identity in World War I* (Cambridge and New York: Cambridge University Press, 1979); Paul Moeyes, *Siegfried Sassoon: Scorched Glory: A Critical Study* (New York: St. Martin's Press, 1997); W. H. R. Rivers, *Instinct and the Unconscious*, 2nd edition (Cambridge: Cambridge University Press, 1924 [1920]); W. H. R. Rivers, "The Psychological Factor," in W. H. R. Rivers, ed., *Essays on the Depopulation of Melanesia* (Cambridge: Cambridge University Press, 1922); W. H. R. Rivers, *Conflict and Dream* (New York: Harcourt, Brace, 1923); W. H. R. Rivers, *Psychology and Ethnology* (New York: Harcourt, Brace, 1926); Siegfried Sassoon, *Sherston's Progress* (London: Faber and Faber, 1936); Ben Shephard, *A War of Nerves: Soldiers and Psychiatrists in the Twentieth Century* (Cambridge, MA: Harvard University Press, 2001); Richard Slobodin, *W. H. R. Rivers: Pioneer Anthropologist, Psychiatrist of the Ghost Road* (Gloucestershire, UK: Sutton, 1997 [1978]); George Stocking Jr., *Malinowski, Rivers, Benedict and Others: Essays on Culture and Personality* (Madison: University of Wisconsin Press, 1986); Allan Young, *The Harmony of Illusions* (Princeton: Princeton University Press, 1995).

On medical and psychiatric diagnoses that went into and out of fashion in the late nineteenth and early twentieth centuries, see George Frederick Drinka, *The Birth of Neurosis: Myth, Malady, and the Victorians* (New York: Simon and Schuster, 1984); Marijke Gijswijt-Hofstra and Roy Porter, eds., *Cultures of Neurasthenia: From Beard to the First World War* (Amsterdam: Rodopi, 2001); F. G. Gosling, *Before Freud: Neurasthenia and the American Medical Community* (Urbana: University of Illinois Press, 1988); Mark S. Micale, *Approaching Hysteria* (Princeton: Princeton University Press, 1994); Edward Shorter, *From Paralysis to Fatigue: A History of Psychosomatic Illness in the Modern Era* (New York: Free Press, 1993).

On late-nineteenth- and early-twentieth-century attempts to create new forms of psychotherapy, see Henri Ellenberger, *Discovery of the Unconscious* (New York: Basic Books, 1981); Marcel Gauchet and Gladys Swain, *Mad-*

ness and Democracy: The Modern Psychiatric Universe, trans. Catherine Porter (Princeton: Princeton University Press, 1999).

The subject of medical ethics has become a huge one, with everything from textbooks and research monographs to specialized journals. A few books pertinent to *What Really Matters* include Sudhir Anand, Fabienne Peter, and Amartya Sen, eds., *Public Health, Ethics and Equity* (Oxford: Oxford University Press, 2004); Judith Andre, *Bioethics as Practice* (Chapel Hill: University of North Carolina Press, 2002); Charles L. Bosk, *Forgive and Remember: Managing Medical Failure* (Chicago: University of Chicago Press, 1981); Allan Brandt and Paul Rozin, eds., *Morality and Health* (New York: Routledge, 1997); John Broome, *Weighing Lives* (Oxford: Oxford University Press, 2004); Allen Buchanan, Dan Brock, Norman Daniels, and Daniel Wikler, *From Chance to Choice: Genetics and Justice* (Cambridge: Cambridge University Press, 2000); Daniel Callahan, *The Troubled Life* (Washington, DC: Georgetown University Press, 2000); John D. Caputo, *Against Ethics* (Bloomington: Indiana University Press, 1993); Deen K. Chatterjee, *Ethics of Assistance: Morality and the Distant Needy* (Cambridge: Cambridge University Press, 2004); David DeGrazia, *Human Identity and Bioethics* (Cambridge: Cambridge University Press, 2005); Arthur Kleinman, Allan Brandt, and Renée Fox, eds., "Bioethics and Beyond," special issue of *Daedalus*, volume 128, number 4, fall 1999; Thomas W. Pogge, ed., *Global Justice* (London: Blackwell, 2001); Martha Nussbaum and Amartya Sen, eds., *The Quality of Life* (Oxford: Oxford University Press, 1993); Peter Singer, *Rethinking Life and Death: The Collapse of Our Traditional Ethics* (New York: St. Martin's Press, 1994).

For the most recent illustration of the medicalization of ordinary unhappiness and existential angst into mental disorders, see Ronald C. Kessler, Patricia Bergland, et al., "Lifetime Prevalence and Age-of-Onset Distribution of DSM-IV Disorders in the National Comorbidity Survey Replication," *Archives of General Psychiatry* 62 (2005): 593–602 (this influential epidemiological study claims that about half of all Americans will experience mental illness sometime in their lifetime); David Healy, *The Anti-Depressant Era* (Cambridge: Harvard University Press, 1997). For a classic statement in social theory, see Renée C. Fox, "The Medicalization and Demedicalization of American Society," in *Essays in Medical Sociology*, 465–83 (New York: John Wiley, 1979).

On the works and life of Albert Camus, see *The Stranger* (New York: Knopf, 1988 [1942]); *The Plague* (New York: Knopf, 1948 [1947]); *The Fall* (New York: Knopf, 1991 [1956]), *The First Man* (New York: Random House, 1996 [1994]); Herbert Lottmann, *Albert Camus: A Biography* (Corte Madera, CA: Gingko Press, 1979).

On the works and life of Primo Levi, see *Survival in Auschwitz* (New York: Touchstone, 1996 [1958]); *Drowned and the Saved* (New York: Simon and Schuster, 1988 [1986]); Carole Angier, *The Double Bond: Primo Levi, a Biography* (New York: Farrar, Straus and Giroux, 2003).

On the works and life of Emmanuel Lévinas, see his *Totality and Infinity*, trans. Alphonso Lingis (Pittsburgh: Duquesne University Press, 1969); *Otherwise than Being: Or Beyond Essence*, trans. Alphonso Lingis (Pittsburgh: Duquesne University Press, 1998); *Entre Nous*, trans. Michael B. Smith (New York: Columbia University Press, 2000), especially "Useless Suffering"; *Time and the Other*, trans. Richard A. Cohen (Pittsburgh: Duquesne University Press, 1987). See also Robert Bernasconi and David Wood, eds., *The Provocation of Lévinas: Rethinking the Other* (London: Routledge, 1998); and John Llewelyn, *Emmanuel Lévinas: The Genealogy of Ethics* (London: Routledge, 1995).

On William James's use of the idea of "genuine reality," see Linda Simon, *Genuine Reality: A Life of William James* (New York: Harcourt Brace and Co., 1998). See also William James, *Varieties of Religious Experience* (Cambridge: Harvard University Press, 1985 [1902]); William Joseph Gavin, *William James and the Reinstatement of the Vague* (Philadelphia: Temple University Press, 1992); Gerald E. Myers, *Williams James: His Life and Thought* (New Haven: Yale University Press, 1986).

On mentoring and its perils, see Harold Bloom, *The Anxiety of Influence* (Oxford: Oxford University Press, 1975); Takeo Doi, *Understanding Amae: The Japanese Concept of Need-Love* (Kent: Global Oriental, 2005).

On the complexities of authenticity, see Alexander Nehamas, *Virtues of Authenticity* (Princeton: Princeton University Press, 1998); Charles Taylor, *The Ethics of Authenticity* (Cambridge: Harvard University Press, 1991); Lionel Trilling, *Sincerity and Authenticity* (Cambridge: Harvard University Press, 1972).

On witnessing and testimony, see C. A. J. Coady, *Testimony: A Philosophical Study* (Oxford: Clarendon Press, 1992); Veena Das, "Wittgenstein and Anthropology," *Annual Review of Anthropology* 27 (1998): 171–95; Shoshana Felman and Dori Laub, *Testimony: Crises of Witnessing in Literature, Psychoanalysis and History* (London: Routledge, 1992); Lawrence L. Langer, *Holocaust Testimonies: The Ruins of Memory* (New Haven: Yale University Press, 1991).

On moral responsibility in the lives of public intellectuals, see Tony Judt, *The Burden of Responsibility: Blum, Camus, Aron, and the French Twentieth Century* (Chicago: University of Chicago Press, 1998).

On antiheroism, see Victor Brombert, *In Praise of Antiheroes: Figures and Themes in Modern European Literature, 1830–1980* (Chicago: University of Chicago Press, 1999); Stanley Hoffman, "Passion and Compassion: The Glory of Albert Camus," *World Policy Journal*, winter 1995, 85–90.

On the history of extreme social dangers that result from the overreaction of people to perceived threats to what is culturally at stake, see Ian Kershaw, *Hitler*, 2 vols. (New York: Norton, 1999–2000); Catherine Merridale, *Night of Stone: Death and Memory in Russia* (London: Granta Books, 2000); R. I. Moore, "The Inquisitor's Nightmare," *Times Literary Supplement*, February 9, 2001, 10–11.

On pain, see Good et al., eds., *Pain as Human Experience*; Kleinman, *The Illness Narratives*; Kleinman et al., eds., *Social Suffering*; Roselyne Rey, *The History of Pain* (Cambridge, MA: Harvard University Press, 1993); Elaine Scarry, *The Body in Pain: The Making and Unmaking of the World* (New York and Oxford: Oxford University Press, 1985); Susan Sontag, *Regarding the Pain of Others* (New York: Farrar, Straus and Giroux, 2002).

On the lived experience of AIDS, see João Biehl, *Vita: Life in a Zone of Abandonment* (Berkeley: University of California Press, 2005); Farmer, *AIDS and Accusation*; Farmer, Connors, and Simmons, eds., *Women, Poverty and AIDS*; Salmaan Keshavjee et al., "Medicine Betrayed: Hemophilia Patients and HIV in the US," *Social Science and Medicine* 53 (2001): 1081–94; Paul Monette, *Borrowed Time: An AIDS Memoir* (New York: Harcourt Brace Jovanovich, 1988); Abraham Verghese, *My Own Country: A Doctor's Story* (New York: Vintage, 1994); George Whitmore, *Someone Was Here: Profiles in the AIDS Epidemic* (New York: New American Library, 1988).

On religion, medicine, and subjectivity, see William James, *The Varieties of Religious Experience* (Cambridge, MA: Harvard University Press, 1985 [1902]); Georges Bernanos, *The Diary of a Country Priest* (New York: Carroll and Graf, 1937); Linda Barnes et al., eds., *Religion and Healing in America* (New York: Oxford University Press, 2005); John Bowker, *Problems of Suffering in Religions of the World* (Cambridge: Cambridge University Press, 1970); Thomas Csordas, *The Sacred Self* (Berkeley: University of California Press, 1994); John R. Hinnells and Roy Porter, eds., *Religion, Health and Suffering* (London: Kegan Paul International, 1999); C. S. Lewis, *The Problem of Pain* (New York: Collier Books, 1962); Judith Perkins, *The Suffering Self: Pain and Narrative Representation in the Early Christian Era* (London: Routledge, 1995); Wayne Proudfoot, *Religious Experience* (Berkeley: University of California Press, 1985); Dorothee Soelle, *Suffering* (Philadelphia: Fortress Press, 1984).

On critiques of humanitarian assistance and development projects, see Mark Duffield, *Global Governance and the New Wars* (New York: Zed Books, 2001); Arturo Escobar, *Encountering Development: The Making and Unmaking of the Third World* (Princeton, NJ: Princeton University Press, 1995); James Ferguson, *The Anti-Politics Machine: "Development," Depoliticization, and Bureaucratic Power in Lesotho* (Minneapolis: University of Minnesota Press, 1994); Mariella Pandolfi, "Contract of Mutual (In)Difference: Governance and Humanitarian Apparatus in Contemporary Albania and Kosovo," *Indiana Journal of Global Legal Studies* 10, 1 (2003):369–81; "Une souveraineté mouvante et supracoloniale. L'industrie humanitaire dans les Balkans," *Multitudes* 3 (2000): 97–105; Samantha Power, *A Problem from Hell: America and the Age of Genocide* (New York: Perennial, 2003).

On failed and failing states in Africa, see Philip Gourevitch, *We Wish to Inform You That Tomorrow We Will Be Killed with Our Families* (New York: Picador 1999); William Reno, *Warlord Politics in African States* (Boulder, CO: Lynne Rienner, 1998); Paul Richards, *Fighting for the Rainforest: War, Youth, and Resources in Sierra Leone* (Portsmouth, NH: Heinemann, 1996); M. Turshen and C. Twagiramariya, eds., *What Women Do in Wartime* (London: Zed Books, 1998); Carolyn Nordstrom, *Shadows of War* (Berkeley: University of California Press, 2004).

Of biographies that richly describe cultural contexts of moral experience and the struggles of remarkable individuals to lead moral lives, see Myriam Anissimov, *Primo Levi: Tragedy of an Optimist*, trans. Steve Cox (Woodstock, NY: Overlook Press, 1999); W. Jackson Bate, *Samuel Johnson* (New York: Harcourt Brace Jovanovich, 1975); Ronald W. Clark, *Freud: The Man and the Cause* (New York: Random House, 1980); Bernard Crick, *George Orwell: A Life* (Boston: Little, Brown and Co., 1980); Tracy Kidder, *Mountains beyond Mountains: The Quest of Dr. Paul Farmer, a Man Who Would Cure the World* (New York: Random House, 2004); Olivier Todd, *Albert Camus: A Life*, trans. Benjamin Ivry (New York: Alfred A. Knopf, 1997).

The literary works cited in this book with reference to moral experience are W. H. Auden, *Collected Poems* (New York: Vintage International, 1991 [1976]); Joseph Conrad, *Lord Jim* (New York: Penguin, 1988); Joseph Conrad, *Victory* (New York: Penguin, 1996); Frances Cornford, "Youth," in *Poems* (Cambridge: Bowes and Bowes, 1910); Henry James, "The Middle Years," in *The Turn of the Screw and the Aspern Papers* (New York: Penguin, 1986); Franz Kafka in a letter to Max Brod describing Robert Klopstock, dated February 1, 1921, in Leo A. Lensing, "Franz Would Be with Us Here," *Times Literary Supplement*, February 28, 2003, 13–15; Imre Kertész, *Kaddish for an Unborn Child*, trans. Christopher Wilson and Katharina Wilson (Evanston, IL: Northwestern University Press, 1997 [1990]); Philip Larkin, *Collected Poems* (New York: Farrar, Straus and Giroux, 2004); John Greenleaf Whittier, "Barbara Frietchie," in *Complete Poetical Works of John Greenleaf Whittier* (Boston: Houghton Mifflin, 1895).

Books are not the only, or even the main, source of knowledge about moral experience; films offer some of the most deeply arresting illustrations (as do plays and opera). In the hauntingly powerful Brazilian film classic *Central Station* (1998, Walter Salles Jr.), for example, Doña Dora, a working-class retired teacher who now lives by writing letters for illiterate travelers passing through Rio's central train station—letters that she cynically either fails to mail or actually tears up—is so concerned with the limited income she realizes to support a lifestyle that frustrates her that she seeks to sell an orphan to operators of a ring that trades in children. Forced by a friend to confront the evil of what she has done, she frees the boy and accompanies him on a picaresque quest to find his absent father. In traveling by bus, pilgrims' van, and foot from Rio to Brazil's impoverished northeast, Doña Dora first loses her money, then her commitment, then the boy himself, only to undergo a religious and moral transformation that will take her and the boy to reunion with his adult brothers and then send her back, as a new, remoralized person, on the bus to Rio. I find this film illustrative of some of the key ideas in this book, for example, local worlds of suffering; the dangers of social experience, including our own participation in dangerous acts; the defeats and limits of everyday life; the possibilities of moral-emotional transformation for self and others; the place of moral responsibility and imagination in our lives; and the divided sense that where the world is taking us is both ominous and hopeful—the former requiring protest and resistance on our part, the latter readiness for change. I'm sure readers have their own list of such films. Others in my list include *Hiroshima Mon Amour* (1959, Alain Resnais); *Floating in the Air Followed by the Wind* (1976, Gunther Pfaff); *The Blue Kite* (1993, Zhuangzhuang Tian); *The Wall* (1998, Alain Berliner); *All About My Mother* (1999, Pedro Almodóvar); *It's My Life* (2001, Brian Tilley); *From the Other Side* (2002, Chantal Akerman); *Beijing Bicycle* (2002, Xiaoshuai Wang); *The Pianist* (2002, Roman Polanski); *Three Rooms of Melancholia* (2005, Pirjo Honkasalo).

Acknowledgments

This book has been many (too many) years in the making. I initially wrote several detailed historical and philosophical chapters meant to frame the life stories included here. I later decided those chapters were too academic for the book I wanted and needed to write, and so I put them aside. Nonetheless, I fear they were a burden to the final year of life of Joan Gillespie, my devoted friend and longtime assistant. For this I am regretful, but for the rare privilege of working with her, I will always be deeply grateful.

My current assistant, Marilyn Goodrich, picked up the threads and pieces and typed the entire manuscript into the computer, including multiple revisions and edits. I thank her wholeheartedly for her skilled work and warm and responsive personal style. I also acknowledge the contributions of several graduate student research assistants: Erin Fitz-Henry, Jesse Grayman, and especially Pete Benson, as well as assistance from Cris Paul.

The chapter on W. H. R. Rivers benefited greatly from some days spent in the Master's Lodge at Trinity College, Cambridge, England. For that opportunity I thank my colleague Amartya Sen, then master of the college. At Cambridge, the reference librarians at the University Library were good enough to help me access the relevant materials in the A. C. Haddon Collection on Rivers's life and intellectual career. I also benefited from discussions in Cambridge with Anita Herle and Sir Martin Roth.

I have presented earlier versions of the introduction and epilogue as well as the chapter on Rivers in a number of seminars: the Friday Morning Research Seminar in Medical Anthropology at Harvard; the Faculty Colloquium of the Department of Social Medicine, Harvard Medical School; the History of Psychoanalysis Dinner Seminar at Harvard's Faculty Club; Amherst College, Dickinson College, Williams College, the University of California at Berkeley, Stanford, Princeton, Columbia, the University of California at Davis, the University of California at Los Angeles, Case Western Reserve, Johns Hopkins, the State University of New York Downstate Medical Center, Mt. Sinai Medical School, University of Manchester, University College London, and the Chinese University of Hong Kong, among other venues. I acknowledge with great thanks the importance of the responses of members of these audiences to the working out of the ideas in this book. I must acknowledge the assistance of a large group of colleagues and friends whose names are simply too numerous to list. They must each know how much I have learned from their responses to this work, and how much I value their support.

I had forgotten how difficult it is for an academic, and a highly specialized one at that, to write for a wide audience, projecting complex ideas and findings into the space of educated conversations. Tim Bartlett, Kate Hamill, and Peter Ginna have been extraordinary in facilitating clear and direct prose and an accessible message.

It is said that when he broke down psychologically in the midst of his studies of the workings of human societies, the great German sociologist Max Weber was asked why he spent so much time and put in such effort at understanding troubling human conditions. His answer supposedly was that he wanted to see how much he could endure. This project has been a test of my own endurance. Perhaps it has even been more than I could endure. That I didn't break down (though I came close) must be due to the great love and assistance I have received from my family, to whom I dedicate *What Really Matters*.

Index